HOMELESSNESS
IN THE EUROPEAN UNION

Social and Legal Context
of Housing Exclusion in the 1990s

Fourth Research Report
of the European Observatory on
Homelessness

Dr. Dragana Avram
Brussels 1995

FEANTSA

Published with the support of the European Commission.

This report has been written by an independent expert. Its content cannot be considered to reflect the opinion of the European Commission.

Koninklijke Bibliotheek Cataloging in Publication Data
Avramov, Dragana
Homelessness in the European Union
p. 196
1. Homelessness. 2. Housing exclusion. 3. Right to housing.
Published by FEANTSA, 1 rue Defacqz, B-1050 Brussels, Belgium
Tel.: 32-2-538.66.69   Fax: 32-2-539.41.74

Cover page Hors Jeu "Transfert Couleur"

ISBN 90-75529-01-5

ACKNOWLEDGEMENT

This book builds on the research of features and the extent of homelessness carried out for four years by the network of the European Observatory on Homelessness sponsored by the European Commission, and, on the excellent job which National Correspondents have done in 1994. Thanks are due to the Executive Committee and FEANTSA's President Brian Harvey for offering me the challenge of an intellectually rewarding task. I appreciated the critical reading of the manuscript and suggestions made by the members of the Scientific Committee.

It has been a pleasure to work with the Secretariat of FEANTSA and Catherine Parmentier, Secretary General. The book owes much to the serene atmosphere of cooperation which stems from the dedication to the work, commitment to the cause, and intellectual curiosity of FEANTSA's staff.

Brussels, 1995   Dragana Avramov

TABLE OF CONTENTS

Chapter 2

HOMELESSNESS: BREACH OF THE SOCIAL CONTRACT 65

LIST OF TABLES AND GRAPHS

EUROPEAN OBSERVATORY ON HOMELESSNESS:
Research Programme and the Transnational Report

Since 1991 The European Federation of National Organizations working with the Homeless (FEANTSA) has been in charge of the European Observatory on Homelessness.

The Observatory was set up with the aim to:

- Provide information and analyze the social phenomenon of homelessness;
- Analyze trends in the number and characteristics of the homeless population;
- Analyze the relationship between needs of homeless for services and assistance, and available provisions;
- Analyze determinants of homelessness;
- Assess future trends in homelessness;
- Monitor national policies relevant for homeless and evaluate their impact on homelessness;
- Provide information and give assessment of most feasible programmes to assist homeless;
- Monitor the short and long term efficacy of projects for re-integration of homeless;
- Give recommendations about needs for future research, social action and social policies.

The European Observatory on Homelessness works through a network of national correspondents. It publishes every year national reports and a transnational analysis prepared by an independent expert which indicates trends at the European Union level. The list of members of the research network are given in Appendix 1.

The first 1992 transnational report of the Observatory addressed the composition of services available for homeless people and the national policy context of assistance to homeless. The second 1993 report discussed the extent of homelessness and the characteristics of those who find themselves homeless. The third transnational report highlighted the national frameworks of rights as they pertain to homeless people and obstacles to rights and services associated with homelessness. Policy recommendations called for the official recognition of homelessness in all EU states and greater obligations on the public authorities to house homeless people.

The research programme of the Observatory for 1994 was developed within the framework of the long term aims of the Observatory and the research topics developed and partly implemented in 1993. Three issues were focused in the 1994 research:

- Right to adequate housing and access to housing for homeless and badly housed people;
- Trends and characteristics of homelessness;
- Models of good practice of reintegration into housing.

The fourth 1995 comparative research report includes findings and policy implications of the analysis of the social and legal background of housing exclusion. It highlights the social and legislative context of policy making and administration of policy decisions pertaining to the right to housing of homeless and badly housed people. The call for action is based on the analysis of the discrepancy between the statement of intent to combat housing exclusion and the actual access to housing available to people unable to compete on the housing market.

The transnational research report builds on the research reports on homelessness in 1994 prepared by national correspondents and on relevant literature given in the list of references. The list of research reports and other working documents available from FEANTSA which were consulted during the preparation of the comparative analysis are given in Appendix 2.

2

INTRODUCTION

The cumulative effect of research, the visible presence of people sleeping rough in Europe's cities, the vigour of the public debate between important social actors, general public, state authorities, and the call for action by the homeless people themselves, non governmental organizations, trade unions, press, religious institutions, eminent public figures, is reflected in the growing awareness that homelessness is a social problem. The public debate is contributing to the change in the perception and interpretation of social processes leading to extreme housing exclusion. The public concern for the devastating effect of homelessness for individuals and the society as a whole reflects increased awareness of the social risks, and a growing sense of individual isolation and system inadequacy. The call for action to remove structural obstacles to access to decent housing, and to prevent extreme housing exclusion and assist homeless people once poverty and lack of community care have taken their toll, is addressed in the first place to the principal executive offices of a nation, but also to the international community.

The ultimate aim of our analysis of the social and legal context of homelessness in the European Union is to contribute to the perception and understanding of housing exclusion and homelessness as serious social problems in the prosperous economies.

The immediate aim is to illustrate the discrepancy between norms defining the scope of political, juridical and social action to combat housing exclusion, and the social reality of homelessness in the Member States. Our analysis focuses on the discrepancy between norms, values and commitments underlying the right to adequate housing as defined in international law and in the domestic legislation, and the provision of means to enhance access to housing to low-income groups.

The first chapter addresses the social process of realization of the right to housing from the statement of intent, through the establishment of the right to housing, provision of means, monitoring of implementation, to the affirmation and reaffirmation of principles in order to maintain acquired rights. Major standard-setting mechanisms of the United Nations, Council of Europe, and European Union, and statements of intent to enhance the right to housing in the domestic legislation, are dealt with in the first section. As individual claims to a home cannot be made on the basis of statements of intent or programme parts of a country's constitution, the introduction of principles into the domestic legislation marks the passage from the acknowledgement of ethical norms and just claims to the establishment of the right to housing. This issue is addressed in the section on positive law where the degree of the establishment of the right to housing as a legally enforceable claim in the Member States is scrutinized.

Establishment of the right to housing may be recognized as an important step forward in combatting exclusion because of the non-discretionary nature of legal rights which guarantee objectivity of treatment. However, the critical measure of the degree of public commitment goes beyond legal provisions and entails the provision of means, more particularly financial resources, to enhance access to adequate housing. The preliminary illustration of the discrepancy between norms and the provision of means is given through the illustration of the limited scope of legal rights under conditions of inadequate provision of means and the continuous attempts to limit or abolish rights already acquired.

The condition of homeless people, their extreme marginalization in temporary shelters and the analysis of factors of structurally induced housing exclusion, provide a full scale illustration of the discrepancy between the normative sphere and the social reality.

The right to adequate housing as defined in the international standard-setting mechanisms and national legislations goes far beyond the concept of the right to shelter. Thus, the analysis of housing exclusion pursued in Chapter 2 addresses different degrees of housing exclusion and housing stress of badly housed people as well as of those who have no home. Estimates of the number of homeless people and those living under severe housing stress due to overcrowding and substandard accommodation are given in this chapter. Characteristics of homeless people who turn to the public and voluntary organizations for shelter, illustrate the increasing vulnerability of particular population sub-groups such as young adults and women.

4

The social context of homelessness and housing exclusion is given in Chapter 3. Background factors are analyzed under the framework of demographic changes, features of the housing stock and the magnitude of social exclusion. Affordability and quality of low-cost housing and proximate determinants precipitating the trajectory into homelessness are addressed in this chapter.

The impact of value systems on the perception of homelessness and the analysis of the functional basis of social solidarity in increasingly more complex societies provide the theoretical framework for the interpretation of policy implications of research findings. The evaluation of preventive and responsive policies to deal with housing exclusion and homelessness serves as the basis in Chapter 4 for the call for action to bridge the gap between the desirable, the actual and the possible.

The aims to highlight the right to housing as a legal principle, to evaluate the discrepancy between the normative sphere and the actual access to housing by the homeless and badly housed people, and to analyze background factors and determinants of homelessness and housing exclusion, necessitated a multidisciplinary approach. The research departs from the content analysis of relevant United Nations, Council of Europe and European Union Declarations, Covenants, Recommendations and Agreements which address the right to housing. The analysis of the incorporation of the right to housing in domestic legislation and means made available to access the right is partly based on the information provided in National Reports for the European Observatory on Homelessness and largely on personal research. In order to estimate the magnitude of the population excluded from adequate housing and determinants of housing exclusion we have used national data collected by service providers and local authorities, selected data from population and household censuses and most pertinent medium and small-scale surveys. The analysis of background factors is based on data provided by national statistical offices and scientific and policy oriented research reports on demography, housing and poverty.

Chapter 1

HUMAN RIGHTS AND THE INHERENT DIGNITY OF (HOMELESS) PERSON

Is the right to a home one of basic human rights? Is the right to a home established in the domestic legislation? Should homeless and badly housed people receive preferential treatment to overcome the structural obstacles to the access to the right? These are the three key questions we will address in this Chapter.

The principle of cooperation based on solidarity is institutionalized in the advanced welfare states and its functional utility is generally recognized. Solidarity implies transfers of resources and services between individuals, between social groups and between generations. What, however, is frequently disputed is which human needs should be recognized as a matter of universal right, and whether general human rights need to be complemented by specific rights of the poor.

The concept of rights to which individuals are entitled for the sole fact that they are human beings, evolved from the perception of the intrinsic value of human beings and the functional advantages of institutionalized solidarity. The right to dignified living is the nucleus from which principles for the identification of the content of basic social rights stem out. The path from the identification of the right, to the explicit recognition to all citizens and establishment of institutional guarantees of access to the right, are part of a durable process of negotiation and political pressure of different interest groups in increasingly more complex societies.

1.1. NON-EXISTENCE OF RIGHTS VERSUS NON-RESPECT OF RIGHTS

In order to assess whether the right to a home exists or not, we need to clarify the concept of rights and to identify the social process of the establishment of the right to housing. It may be less useful to embark on the ambiguous discussion about the different "nature" of civil and social rights, or about negative and positive rights, than to clarify the content of the concepts and the dynamic interdependence of components of the social process of the realization of rights. The concept of rights encompasses three key dimensions which *inter alia* define their scope and instruments of implementation:

- right as an ethical or moral quality that constitutes the ideal of moral propriety;
- right as something to which one has a just claim;
- legally enforceable claim, a capacity or privilege the enjoyment of which is secured to a person by law.

As an ideal, the right to a home may be considered as a derived right from the right to a personal, independent, dignified living and is a constitutive component of international law. The right to a dwelling may be recognized as an inseparable part of basic rights and as a precondition for access to rights conducive to dignified living. But, the lack of implementing instruments of international law and of political declarations implies that the statement of intent remains the maximum scope of the right. Within a more binding legislative framework, that of sovereign states, the right to housing as a privilege to which one may have a just claim, is recognized as the right of legal residents and not as a universal right. When the right to housing is incorporated into domestic standard-setting instruments, only the nationals, and some categories of legally resident foreigners, are identified as persons who may have a just claim to a home.

The right to housing as an ethical quality is acknowledged in major international standard-setting mechanisms adopted or ratified by the Member States of the European Union. Thus, even when it is not explicitly formulated at the national level as the statement of intent, it may be argued that states have made a political commitment to the community of nations to enhance the right to dignified living conditions.

The concept of the right to housing as a legal principle and an enforceable claim is recognized only by a minority of European Union states. As a legally enforceable claim, the right to housing entails the commitment of political, juridical and financial means. It requires a clear identification of target groups, of instruments of positive discrimination and degrees of urgency of implementation.

The line of interaction between the evolution of general principles and social institutions, entails recognition of rights and respect of rights. When comparing principles of international law as standard-setting mechanisms and the national legislations establishing rights and allocating means, we may distinguish two basic situations which generate housing exclusion: non-existence of the right to housing because the right has not been defined as a legal principle in the domestic legislation, and non-respect of the right because means are not provided.

The mere identification of the right to housing and enumeration of supporting rights does not suffice to combat exclusion. But, structural obstacles cannot be removed unless the right to a home is identified, explicitly recognized to all citizens and institutionally guaranteed.

The constitutive components of the social process of realization of rights include:
- statement of intent;
- establishment of rights;
- provision of means;
- monitoring of implementation;
- affirmation and reaffirmation of principles in order to exert moral and political pressure to maintain acquired rights.

We will pursue the analysis of the levels of recognition and the degrees of implementation of the right to housing along the continuum of the social process leading to the accomplishment of rights in the Member States. We will particularly focus on the relationship between the political and juridical commitments and the allocation of resources.

Every right, as an ethical quality and/or as a legally enforceable claim, involves various attributes such as adherence to a set of principles or to a duty. A right as a social quality cannot be separated from requirements which individuals are expected to fulfil and duties they have to comply with. The principle is unquestionable. What, however, needs to be permanently scrutinized is the degree to which the requirements are equitable. Rules and terms of competition on the national housing market and access to resources for low-income groups are the two key variables of equity. Non-respect of rights does not result only from the non-allocation or insufficient allocation of resources. It is frequently rooted in the inequitable allocation of available resources so that solidarity does not reach the most needy, the homeless and badly housed people. Thus, in order to evaluate the impact of structural features of exclusion from adequate housing we need to analyze the key aspects of the prevailing housing and social policies as they affect low-income groups.

1.2. JURIDICAL INSTRUMENTS AND THE IMPLEMENTATION OF THE RIGHT TO HOUSING

Advantages of the juridical protection of homeless and badly housed people rest in the non-discretionary nature of legal rights which guarantee objectivity of treatment of homeless people, minimal standards of adequacy of dwellings, and security of tenure.

In some European Union countries, a commitment to the right to adequate housing made in the domestic legislation does not go further than the statement of intent. Such is the case in Greece, Spain, Italy, or Portugal where the social policy and the provision of means do not accompany the political and juridical commitment consistently or effectively. In others, Belgium, Germany, France, Ireland or the United Kingdom, a body of enabling legislative measures addressing the right to housing or the condition of homelessness has been passed. In these countries the laws are, to a varying degree, accompanied by instruments of welfare policy and measures. In Denmark, Luxembourg and the Netherlands the right to housing is not specifically recognized in the legislation as an individual entitlement. But, in these countries the political consensus that it is in the interest of the society to provide housing for every household is operationalized through a generous comprehensive social policy. In Denmark, Luxembourg and the Netherlands, the right to dignified living is protected by the comprehensive preventative and responsive social policy and measures which encompass specific provisions for people in need of housing assistance.

Our aim is not to analyze the legal principles *per se*, nor the legal instruments in their own right, but rather to evaluate the extent of overall commitment of the Member States to the realization of the right to housing. Our analysis of the codification of the right to a home in international law, in the European Charters, and in national legislations, aims only at providing the background for the analysis of the efficacy of instruments used. Furthermore, our aim is not to pursue a legislative approach to housing in general, nor to look at housing rights of the population as a whole. We will not analyze housing rights since legislation in the housing sector deals with a very broad range of regulations, from standards of construction, set up of building companies and terms of their operation, to housing transactions and payment conditions. We will focus on the right to housing as it may affect individual titulars, and will pursue the analysis of provisions and instruments made available to low-income groups and people in need of community care so that they can acquire a home and stay in their home.

We will look at the key political, juridical and financial means which the Member States put into practice in order to provide access to the right to housing. The political commitment to protect the most vulnerable members of the society operates within a system of short and long-term priorities of the authorities. Under the prevailing economic system, the most pertinent political commitment is that to welfare provisions based on both contributory and on non-contributory schemes. Juridical means include commitments made at international, regional and national levels to promote human rights both in their civil and social dimension. The commitment of financial resources for minimum subsistence means, low-cost housing, and rent subsidies, may be considered as the ultimate measure of governmental adherence to established principles and priorities.

1.2.1. Statement of intent

A statement of intent formulated by the government is an important standard-setting instrument. It is generally recognized as a valuable impetus to the social process of implementation of rights. The acknowledgement of the right to housing as one of basic human rights and the explicit formulation of the intention of governments to promote access to the right to housing marks a significant political and juridical step towards its establishment. Normative standards pertaining to the right to housing are integrated in the universal, regional, sub-regional and national political and juridical instruments. In order to evaluate the degree of commitment to the right to housing we will give an overview of aims, strategies and instruments of the most pertinent United Nations, Council of Europe, European Union, and Member State's acts propagating the right to housing.

1.2.1.1. United Nations

The right to adequate housing is embodied in numerous international human rights texts. The first important document to codify the right was the Universal Declaration of Human Rights (UN General Assembly, 1948). The Declaration builds upon the premise that basic human needs should be recognized as rights, and promotes the concept of human dignity as a legal principle:

> "Everyone has the right to a standard of living adequate for the health and wellbeing for himself and his family, including food, clothing, **housing**[1], and medical care and necessary social services, and the right to security in the event of unemployment, sickness, disability, widowhood, old age or other lack of livelihood in circumstances beyond his control." (Article 21.1)

The Declaration is a consensus on principles underlying the realization of the civil, economic, social and cultural rights. It is a standard-setting mechanism which affirms key moral norms and recognizes the realization of the right as a moral norm. The Declaration asserts the principle that human rights are indivisible and that civil and social rights are interdependent. It recognizes that the right to dignified living builds upon adequate living conditions, essential components of which are enumerated in Article 21 paragraph 1. Adequate standard of living, as defined by the Declaration, includes housing as one of its cornerstones. Thus, the right to adequate housing may be generally considered as a right derived from the universal right to an adequate standard of living.

In the course of almost half a century of United Nations activities, 12 different declarations, recommendations or covenants explicitly recog-

---

[1] Underlined by the author D. Avramov.

nize the right to adequate housing (Centre for Human Rights, 1993). In addition to the International Labour Organization Recommendation on Worker's Housing (ILO, 1961) which defines the objective of providing

"adequate and decent housing accommodation .... to all workers and their families" (Recommendation 115),

the Declaration on Social Progress and Development (UN General Assembly, 1969) addresses the issue of "the material and spiritual standard of living of all members of society". Article 10 defines one of the main goals of development policies:

"The provision for all, particularly persons in low-income groups and large families, of adequate housing and community services." (Article 10)

Other relevant international law instruments include the International Convention on the Elimination of All Forms of Racial Discrimination (UN General Assembly, 1965) and the protection of specific population groups.

The Universal Declaration of Human Rights is based on the consensus that basic human rights are entitlements to which all human beings may have a just claim. The premise of universality may seemingly make the identification of specific population target groups redundant. From a theoretical point of view it may be argued that identification of target groups is not necessary since universal encompasses particular. From the practical point of view, however, equitable access to the right may require identification of target groups and their preferential treatment. The principle of equality in rights does not automatically imply equity. As long as there is structural discrimination which exposes individuals to particular social vulnerability, policies and measures of positive discrimination or preferential treatment are needed to enhance the principle of equal opportunity. Indeed, the United Nations have adopted the principle of positive discrimination to counterbalance the structural obstacles, and have identified several target groups. A series of specific UN Conventions, Declarations and Recommendations are targeted at the undeserved population groups.

Refugees (UN, 1951), children (UN, 1959; 1989), workers (ILO, 1961), women (UN, 1979), older workers (ILO, 1980), migrant workers (UN,

1990) minorities (UN, 1991), indigenous peoples (UN, 1993) are target groups of policies to overcome discrimination and secure protection by means of explicit reference to housing conditions. The Convention on the Elimination of All Forms of Discrimination Against Women in Art. 14.2 (h) specifically mentions housing as a component of adequate living conditions. The Convention on the Rights of the Child in Art. 27.3 refers to the right to housing assistance for parents and other responsible for the child so that the rights of the child can be implemented.

Homeless and badly housed people have not, up to now, been identified as a specific target group. In numerous United Nations instruments housing is generally identified as an integral part of development policies. The declarations and covenants name housing as a component of dignified living conditions, but do not identify homeless people as a vulnerable group in need of particular protection. The furthest the UN General Assembly has gone is to express:

> "its deep concern that millions of people do not enjoy the right to adequate housing." (Resolution 41/146, 1986)

The Vancouver declaration on Human Settlements (UN, 1976) reiterates the principles of the Universal Declaration of Human Rights and calls for human settlement policies to be in conformity with universal rights. It explicitly names the right to adequate housing as a basic human right:

> "Adequate shelter and services are a basic human right which places an obligation on governments to ensure their attainment by all people, beginning with direct assistance to the least advantaged through guided programmes of self-help and community action. Governments should endeavour to remove all impediments hindering attainment of these goals. Of special importance is the elimination of social and racial segregation, inter alia, through the creation of better balanced communities which blend different social groups, occupations, housing and amenities." (Section III, 8)

Since the Vancouver Conference, numerous UN resolutions have reiterated the right to adequate housing, the need to take appropriate measures and to ensure periodic review of the implementation of the right by the Member States. The United Nations have thus exhausted available instruments. As is known, international law does not (yet) have the legal instruments to specify the concrete rights and duties evolving from the formal recognition of the right to housing. In addition to the moral commitment made by the governments in different declarations and recommendations, covenants are the strongest UN instruments binding countries which have ratified it. The process of implementation of the right to adequate housing has, indeed, passed from the declarative acknowledgement of the right to the recognition of the right in the International Covenant on Economic, Social and Cultural Rights (UN General Assembly, 1966) and monitoring of compliance by the signatories.

The International Covenant on Economic, Social and Cultural Rights has a stronger legally binding character than the Universal Declaration on Human Rights and thus the inclusion of the housing clause marks an important step forward in the establishment of the right to housing. The Covenant ratified by 106 states (Centre for Human Rights, 1993) including all European Union countries, reiterates the right to adequate standard of living and directly names housing as one requirement. At the international level the state compliance with the undertaken commitments is monitored by the Committee on Economic, Social and Cultural Rights.

Sanctions for non-compliance are not anticipated. The ways individual countries interpret and incorporate into the domestic legislation international commitments made in the Covenant vary considerably. Indeed, the interpretation of the meaning of clauses and juridical weight of internationally ratified principles is by no means uniform in the European Union countries (Vogel-Polsky, 1992). The binding nature of the Covenant is translated in Belgium in the acknowledgement by the Court of Arbitration of its competence in the monitoring of the implementation of the Covenant (Fierens, 1995). This may be cited as an example of good practice in domestic monitoring of compliance with recognized principles.

It is generally acknowledged that housing as a component of economic, social and cultural rights can only be realized progressively and that the implementation of the right is dependant upon the availability of economic resources and their allocation to identified target groups. The obligation to commit resources does not remain entirely vague, nor does it settle for symbolic inputs, as each state party to the Covenant agreed to undertake steps "to the maximum of its available resources" (Article 2.1).

1.2.1.2. Council of Europe

Member States of the Council of Europe have made a joint commitment to the universal principles of human rights by adopting the European Convention for the Protection of Human Rights and Fundamental Freedoms (Council of Europe, 1950 and 1953). However, the regional implementation of principles adopted at the universal level, was associated to a narrower establishment of human rights. The Convention has essentially focused on civil rights and has omitted to develop clauses addressing economic, social and cultural rights. One may go so far as to affirm that the regional Convention has breached the principle of indivisibility of rights already affirmed in the Universal Declaration. One set of rights is addressed in the Convention, another in the Social Charter, reflecting not only different conceptualization of rights, but also different level of commitments and mechanisms of control of their implementation.

The Convention makes no reference to the right to adequate housing. It is only the European Social Charter (Council of Europe, 1961 and 1965), which was ratified by all European Union States, which mentions housing. However, there is no reference to the universal right to housing, but only to the right of the family to social, legal and economic protection. Article 16 anticipates the provision of family housing which may be interpreted as a measure to protect the family's right to housing.

It may be argued that a number of articles pertaining to the security of the person and respect for the private home in the European Convention, and the protection against physical and moral danger in the European Social Charter, may be very broadly related to the principle of security of a home. But, the clauses aim at reinforcing the rights of those with a home rather than at providing access to a home to those whose right to the privacy (of a home) is altogether breached. Indeed, the Commission on Human Rights has always defended the position that Article 8 which deals with the respect for family life and privacy of a home, does not impose an obligation on States to provide housing. The fact is that when states adopted regional instruments which are somewhat closer to mandatory implementation than the UN declarations and covenants, they

16

opted out of a binding commitment to the establishment of the right to housing.

The recommendation to embody the right to housing in existing legal instruments, particularly in the European Convention on Human Rights was recently reiterated in the Resolution 244 of the Standing Conference of Local and Regional Authorities of Europe (1993). The Final declaration adopted at the end of the International Conference on Social Housing, the Homeless and the Poorly-Housed in Europe states:

> "implementing the right to housing, a fundamental right of
> any individual, is a priority duty of society as a whole and
> a collective obligation of public authorities at all levels."
> (Section V.3)

Similar declarations and recommendations have been advanced to the Council in other instances, more particularly when policies to combat social exclusion were discussed. One of the more recent recommendations No. R (93)1 of the Committee of Ministers to Member States Regarding Effective Access to the Law and to Justice for the Very Poor expresses concern for the marginalized and excluded, recalls the principle of indivisibility of human rights and reaffirms the principle that civil and political rights cannot be effective unless economic, social and cultural rights are equally protected. Thus, we may expect the right to housing approach to remain on the political agenda of the Council of Europe.

1.2.1.3. European Union

The right to housing has not been on the policy agenda of the European Union. Treaties and agreements which serve as legal basis for the Community action make no reference to the right to housing or to housing conditions of the poor. The Treaty of Rome (1958), the European Single Act (1985), the Maastricht Treaty (1992), do not establish provisions for the legal competence of the Commission of the European Union in the domain of housing. Thus, the institutional functioning of the Commission is based on the interpretation of the principle of subsidiarity which recognises the sole competence for dealing with housing issues to the Member States. Housing is dealt with within the framework of national housing policies. The decision not to include housing in the field of competence of the European Commission was explicitly affirmed by the twelve Ministers for Housing, when questions pertaining to housing exclusion were addressed at their first informal meeting in December 1989.

The lack of competence, on the one hand, and the specific interpretation of the principle of subsidiarity, on the other, imply that there are no European legislative instruments to acknowledge and monitor the implementation of the right to housing. In other words, there are no regional standard-setting mechanisms to fill in the gap between the universal declaration and national (non)compliance.

The Social Chapter, annexed to the Maastricht Treaty as a protocol and an agreement on Social Policy, adopted by eleven Member States (the United Kingdom opted out) does not mention the right to housing and identifies only the general objective of adequate social protection from exclusion.

Some Community actions, involving modest means to complement a few national housing projects, have however, been implemented. Programmes, such as Poverty III, LEDA, ERGO had a small housing component. Other programmes included housing for coal and steel workers, access to housing for the handicapped, and improvement of housing conditions of legally resident migrant workers. Building of homes for the workers in the steel and mining sectors was facilitated by the Union which allocated long-term loans at one percent interest rate. Since 1954 some 200,000 homes for steel and mining workers have been built, mainly in France and Germany. A pilot project in London aims at reviving poorly maintained large housing estates and council houses in eight run down areas of the city. Similarly, large council estates in Marseille are at the core of an experimental project to generate economic activity for the local population and to renovate housing. Projects in London and Marseille benefitted from the financial support from the European Social Fund (Commission of the European Communities, 1992).

Within the framework of Commission's programmes, a housing component may be identified as a tool for achieving specific economic aims. The focus of Community actions was rather on generating employment than housing the poor. It may be said that a housing component has been a by-product of programmes to create local employment and to revive economically degraded urban areas. The programmes did not include a specific task of housing the homeless.

The Green Paper (Commission of the European Communities, 1993), in which social policy options for the Union are outlined and priorities identified, is the most important consultative document on burning social issues. In it, however, the Commission does not acknowledge homelessness as a severe social problem. Two un-commented photographs, of a woman pushing her belongings in a super-market trolley and of a man with a bottle in the pocket of his jacket sleeping in a doorway (Green Paper, p. 15 and 44), are the only indirect reference to homelessness in the European Union.

The White Paper on European Social Policy (Commission of the European Communities, 1994) which provides the framework for the Union's action, envisages the promotion of social integration of all by means of social policy and social protection. In Chapter 6 the most vulnerable are identified as people excluded from social and economic life, young people, long-term unemployed, disabled and older people (Article 12). Homelessness, as the extreme manifestation of housing and socio-economic exclusion, and homeless people excluded from basic human rights are not specifically mentioned. Chapter 6 which addresses social policy and social protection for all does acknowledge the multidimensional nature of exclusion and links the process "also to housing conditions" (Article 15). A second reference to housing is made in Article 20:

> "Housing is also a key issue in combating social exclusion
> and may also be an important source of new jobs."

It remains unclear whether the clause aims at combating exclusion by housing provisions for all, or whether it just identifies potential job opportunities in one of the sectors of economy. If the focus is on the second, it is questionable whether the construction industry which requires specific professional skills, could provide a significant number of jobs for homeless people.

Promoting construction policies and jobs in the construction industry may, indeed, have an impact on the social and housing policies in the Member States. But, it may by no means be taken for granted that this will facilitate access to housing for homeless and badly housed people. In Chapters 2 and 3 we will document that housing exclusion is fundamentally associated to policies underlying investment into social housing and to the levels of social and housing benefits and rent rebates. A sufficient supply in terms of housing units on the free housing market does not suffice. Indeed, needs of people unable to compete for housing on the free housing market can only be met provided equitable redistribution of available resources is ensured through sufficient supply of public housing and preferential access to adequate housing for low-income groups.

1.2.1.4. Member States

The establishment of the right to housing in the constitution as the highest law of the land, represents an important legal foundation for the implementation of the right. The right to housing as a constitutional right is more than a declarative statement of intent. However, the housing clause is generally interpreted as a component of the programme part of the constitution which does not provide a legal basis for individual claims. An individual claim to a home cannot be made in a court of law in any of the Member States exclusively upon constitutional provisions. The measure of the commitment which goes beyond formal recognition lies in the accompanying legislation which guarantees the implementation of the constitutional rights. It involves legal guarantees that social and financial resources will be committed to enable access to the right.

A housing rights clause has been included in the national constitutions of Portugal, Spain, the Netherlands and Belgium. The constitutional right to a dwelling is defined in some constitutions of the German Lander (e.g. Bavaria, Bremen, Berlin, Brandenburg), but the proposal to include the clause in the Federal constitution following the German reunification has not been accepted (Specht-Kittler, 1993). The right to housing is recognized in the legislation of a number of Italian regions which is considered as having a constitutional role (Tosi and Ranci, 1993).

Some jurists argue that even when the right to housing is not explicitly formulated in the constitution it may derive from other constitutional rights in an indirect way and can be explicitly recognized as a right through jurisprudence. Indeed, in the Member States which have a constitution, rights associated to dignified living conditions may be interpreted as an implicit recognition of the right to dignified housing. The view that the right to housing is an implicit right has been repeatedly supported by the Constitutional Court in Italy, which "in a number of sentences has referred to housing as a fundamental social right" (Tosi and Ranci, 1993).

The fact, however, remains that the right to housing has explicitly been addressed in the constitutions of only four Member States. All the four have chosen not to implement the right to housing as an individual entitlement solely on the basis of the constitutional dispositions.

In the European Union countries which have enshrined the right to housing in their constitution, reference is made to quality housing and not just to housing which could be interpreted as any kind of temporary shelter or sub-standard accommodation. Concepts used are "proper housing", "adequate dwelling", "satisfactory housing", or "decent housing". The constitutional clauses defining the right to housing have been included in the constitutions in recent years. The time span of the incorporation in the constitution of the right to housing, ranges between 1976 in Portugal, 1978 in Spain, 1982 in the Netherlands, and 1994 in Belgium. The wording of the housing clause, the scope of the provision and the *de facto* commitment to the implementation of constitutional provisions varies substantially between the Member States.

The clause in the Portuguese constitution states:

> "Everyone shall have the right for himself and his family
> to a dwelling of adequate size satisfying standards of
> hygiene and comfort and preserving personal and family
> privacy." (Article 65.1)[2]

The constitution also defines duties of the state in safeguarding the right by means of housing policy which *inter alia* includes the promotion of home ownership, the establishment of housing co-operatives and the implementation of rents "comparable with family incomes" (Article 65. paragraphs 2 and 3).

---

[2] English language translation taken over from: Legal Provisions on Housing Rights, COHRE, The Netherlands 1994

The Spanish constitution also defines duties of the public authorities to promote conditions and set standards of adequacy of housing and urban planning:

> "All Spaniards have the right to enjoy decent and adequate housing. The authorities shall promote the conditions necessary and establish pertinent norms to make this right effective, regulating the use of land in accordance with the general interest to prevent speculation. The community shall share in the increased values generated by urban activities of public bodies." (Article 47)[3]

The Netherlands constitution does not include a commitment but it briefly defines a programme:

> "It shall be the concern of the authorities to provide sufficient living accommodation." (Article 22.2)[4]

The right to dignified living conditions enshrined in the new Belgian constitution (1994) is accompanied by a series of social rights. The right to decent housing is a right guaranteed by the highest law of the land. The dispositions in Article 23.3 may be summarized as follows:

> "Everyone has the right to enjoy a life in conformity with human dignity. Towards this end, the law, the decree of rules established under article 134 guarantee, taking into account the corresponding obligations, economic, social and cultural rights of which they determine the conditions for their implementation. These rights include, in particular, the right to adequate housing".[5]

Commitment to the right to housing is only one step in the process of establishment of social rights. The constitutional commitment is the product of modern times and its evolved value systems. In the process of realization of social rights the scope of the constitution is generally

---

[3] Ibidem

[4] Ibidem

[5] Cited from: Legal Provisions on Housing Rights, COHRE, The Netherlands 1994

22

to identify principles which, in the second stage, need to be operationalized through laws. Article 23 of the new Belgian constitution explicitly states that constitutional principles must be operationalized. The dynamics of implementation of the political commitment made in the constitution is generally recognized to be dependent on a series of circumstances. The constitutional clauses pertaining to the right to housing, are indeed, understood as principles which at the present time may not be fully attainable, but are considered as societal goals. The constitutional right to work has a similar status. The right may be recognized in principle, but it is acknowledged that full employment cannot be achieved under the current socio-economic establishment.

Therefore, the actual scope of the right to housing cannot be evaluated solely in terms of the formal recognition of the right in the constitution. An insight into other legal and financial provisions, directly and indirectly associated to housing, is indispensable for the assessment of the establishment of rights. In view of scarce legislative and financial commitment and the lack of implementing mechanisms, the maximum scope of the constitutional right to housing in Portugal and Spain is that of a statement of intent. Housing is not a right which citizens may claim on the basis of the constitutional clause. By contrast, in the Netherlands and Belgium the right to housing is implemented through a series of supporting legal provisions and social policy measures, many of which are older than the incorporation of the right to housing in the constitution.

1.2.1.5. Acknowledgement of the right to housing

The right to housing as a legal principle has been directly acknowledged by all European Union States. The political commitment to social rights, which include the provision of adequate housing, was explicitly made in the Universal Declaration of Human Rights to which all Member States abide. The International Covenant on Economic, Social and Cultural Rights, which directly recognizes the right to adequate housing and which is legally binding for the signatories, was ratified by all Members States. Unequivocally, the right to adequate housing is recognized by all member States as one of the basic human rights founded in international law.

However, the operationalization of the right by international regional organizations, such as the Council of Europe and the European Union, is lagging behind. The European Convention on Human rights of 1950 (Council of Europe, 1950) and the subsequent protocols build on the Universal Declaration of Human rights. In the preamble to the Convention an explicit commitment was made to human rights in their totality. However, the Convention does not include a housing clause and the right to housing is not mentioned. Since the right is not there, individual claims cannot be made before the Court of Human Rights.

The European Social Charter defines the right of all persons to social security schemes and medical assistance (Art. 13) but fails to include access to housing for everyone. It does not identify homeless people as target groups in need of special assistance. It does, however, make recourse to positive discrimination by defining families as groups entitled to social, legal and economic protection. As part of the protective scheme "the Contracting Parties undertake to promote....provision of family housing" (Article 16). The positive discrimination towards families in the Social Charter is no doubt a commendable principle. However, other vulnerable groups also need to be identified so that preferential treatment of families in housing provision does not become an instrument of potential discrimination towards single people, unmarried cohabitants, and non-family households. Article 16 of the Council of Europe Social Charter is altogether ambiguous and open to different interpretations. Oliver (1992) points out that the wording of the French version of the Article "alludes to ways of encouraging the construction of housing, but does not recognize a right to housing".

The European Union does not address the right to housing as a legal principle. Under a particular interpretation of the principle of subsidiarity Member States have the exclusive competence for dealing with housing issues.

The international commitments made by the Member States unequivocally confirm that the right to adequate housing has been asserted as a statement of intent. Up to now, four states, Portugal, Spain, the Netherlands and Belgium, have included the right to housing in the programme part of their constitution. Four other states, France, the United Kingdom and Ireland, as well as Belgium, have passed housing laws, which will be discussed in section on the establishment of the right in positive law. We will further pursue our analysis of the process of the establishment of the right through its incorporated in national legislations. In order to assess whether the right to housing has been operationalized we will look at whether, in addition to legal provisions, other means, more particularly financial resources which enable access to the right, are made available.

At this stage we can conclude that the political and juridical commitment to the right to housing as a principle, made by all Member States in international instruments, and by four countries also in their constitution, has two key implications. In the first place, the political commitment made to the community of nations puts an obligation on public authorities to take legislative steps and to allocate appropriate means to progressively enable access to housing to all citizens. In the second place, the acknowledgement of the right to housing is a commitment to a programme which legitimates further political pressure to establish the right to a home as an individual entitlement which may be claimed in a court of law.

1.3. ESTABLISHMENT OF THE RIGHT IN POSITIVE LAW

In order to make a further step towards the establishment of the right to housing as a legal principle, specific housing and social protection laws need to be passed. In these laws, the right to housing may be explicitly recognized to all citizens, or the right may specifically address only access to housing for undeserved groups, such as the poor and homeless.

Legal instruments put in place at a national level for the compliance with the acknowledged right to housing, include positive law and social policy provisions. The advantages of the right to housing approach are multiple. Laws guarantee that principles and values of a society will be institutionalized and implemented on non-discretionary basis. Legal rights guarantee a high degree of permanency relatively independent from short-term political or policy fluctuation. Laws, however, do not suffice to combat housing exclusion. Social policy provisions, more particularly of preventative nature, are the key to the establishment of rights.

Ambiguities of a formal legal approach to rights need to be born in mind for at least two reasons. Firstly, the fact that a law is passed does not automatically imply that it is implemented in an efficient way. Legal provisions, more particularly when they are set up as enabling legislation, are not always accompanied by a relevant allocation of resources. Secondly, responsive laws aimed at dealing with structurally induced consequences of social and housing exclusion may mask the fact that the system does not address the causes. By focusing only on homelessness as an extreme consequence of exclusion, governments may do little to prevent it from occurring on a mass scale. Indeed, in countries where large numbers of people cannot compete on the housing market due to their income insufficiency, an obligation to assist the homeless may be seen as a palliative measure devised to address an outcome of exclusion from adequate housing, rather than its structural causes. By contrast, in countries in which social and housing policy provisions play an important role in preventing homelessness, juridical mechanisms to claim the right, once housing is lost, may be less pertinent and largely redundant.

Thus, legal provisions need to be evaluated in conjunction with social provisions and in terms of their efficacy both in preventing and alleviating consequences of homelessness. Identification of pertinent legislation is only the first step.

1.3.1. Right to housing which specifically addresses the condition of homelessness

Four European Union States, France, the United Kingdom, Ireland and Belgium, have adopted national laws to transform the right to housing into concrete regulations which address the condition of homelessness. The French law asserts clearly and in a detailed manner the right to housing for all citizens and entitlements of people unable to access housing. The United Kingdom legislation does not assert the right to housing as citizen's right, but puts an obligation on the local authority to house some categories of homeless people. The Irish law does not affirm the general right to housing but it defines responsibilities which local authorities are expected to comply with in monitoring homelessness and housing needs. The law passed in Belgium a year before the right to housing was incorporated in the new constitution as a right for all citizens, specifically addressed some social rights of homeless people and defined obligations to provide for them.

France: The explicit recognition of the fundamental right to housing as a target set for the public authorities has been affirmed through numerous instruments in several laws: Quillot (1982), Mermaz (1989), Besson (1990), Delebarre (1991). The first to affirm the right to housing was the law Quillot which aimed at bridging the controversy between economic rentability of housing and its affordability for tenants. The clauses of the 1989 law provided instruments for the protection of tenants. The full affirmation of the legal principle and implementation of dispositions for the realization of the universal entitlement to housing are put into effect in the law passed in 1990 (Lafore, 1993).

The law 90/449 known as the law Besson, aims at implementing the right to housing and is an effective legal guarantee of the entitlement. The law specifies:

> "The guarantee of a right to housing constitutes an interpretation of duty of solidarity for the nation as a whole. Any person or family finding difficulties because of the inability of his resources to meet his needs has the right to collective assistance under conditions fixed by law that will ensure access to decent and independent housing where he can maintain himself." (Article 1)[6]

To implement the right to housing, the local authorities, i.e. departments, are obliged to set up programmes to house disadvantaged persons. The plan must determine needs and required means, and must allocate available resources to needy people. Priority must be given to:

> "persons and families without any accommodation or those threatened by eviction who have nowhere to move, or those living in slums, insalubrious dwellings or improvised accommodation." (Article 4)[7]

The law mandates the establishment of housing solidarity funds through which financial assistance is provided for households facing difficulties in maintaining a home due to income insufficiency. All requests, regard-

---

[6] English language translation taken over from: Legal Provisions on Housing Rights, COHRE, The Netherlands 1994

[7] Translated from French by the author D. Avramov.

less of the income level and the amount of rent arrears must be reviewed. No request can be *a priori* rejected, and applicants have the right to lodge a complaint if unsatisfied with the decision of the local authorities. The law empowers the state and departments to devise effective policies and to facilitate cooperation between social actors and authorities.

United Kingdom: Under Part III of the Housing Act (1985) the legislation of the United Kingdom guarantees a legally enforceable claim to housing to certain population sub-groups. In order to make the right effective, the Act defines obligation of the local housing authorities mandated to provide accommodation for the homeless. The Act specifies the interim duty of local housing authorities to accommodate in case of apparent priority need (Section 63). People are considered to be in priority need if they have dependent children, if the woman is pregnant, if they become homeless through emergency or disaster or are vulnerable due to old age or a handicap.

Three criteria for eligibility for accommodation are foreseen:
- that the applicant is homeless or threatened by homelessness;
- that she/he is not homeless or potentially homeless intentionally;
- that she/he has a priority need.

To ensure a correct interpretation of mandatory obligations and of target groups throughout the state, a Code of Guidance accompanies the Act. Although the Code of Guidance does not have the "weight" of a law, local authorities who ignore its recommendations can be challenged. In the third edition of the Code of Guidance (1991) an attempt was made to secure fair, consistent and good practice among housing authorities and to fill in some gaps in the legislation. Under the Housing Act 1985, local authorities do not have a statutory responsibility to permanently rehouse single homeless people who are not seen to be vulnerable. However, the Code specifies that the authority must at least interview and give assistance to everyone.

Under the Act, duties to persons found to be homeless and to those found to be threatened with homelessness are respectively to "secure that accommodation is made available or does not cease to be available for people it judges to be homeless (or threatened with homelessness) and who are in priority need and who have not made themselves homeless intentionally" (Code of Guidance, 1991). The Code of Guidance suggests that the length of time spent in temporary accommodation should be kept to a minimum whilst permanent accommodation is being secured.

Ireland: The Housing Act (1988) defines responsibilities of local authorities towards homeless and people marginalized on the formal housing market. Local authorities are expected to measure the extent of housing needs, to count the homeless people and to elaborate housing priorities. They do not have an obligation to house homeless people. Homeless people are those for whom:

> "a - There is no accommodation available which, in the opinion of the authority, he, together with any other person who normally resides with him or who might reasonably be expected to reside with him, can reasonably occupy or remain in occupation of, or,
>
> b - He is living in a hospital, country home, night shelter or other such institution, and is so living because he has no accommodation of the kind referred to in the paragraph (a) and he is, in the opinion of the authority, unable to provide accommodation from his own resources." (Section 2)

Under clauses of the Housing Act, the local authorities are obliged to assess the housing needs of vulnerable groups, to establish priorities for accommodation and to assign a proportion of dwellings to housing persons who cannot manage with his/her own resources. An assessment of needs has to be conducted not less frequently than every three years (Sections 9 and 11). The Act defines types of assistance which may be provided to homeless people and gives the authority a wide discretionary power in determining the type of assistance they believe the homeless person requires (Section 10). The housing authorities are empowered to determine whether a claimant is actually homeless. The eligibility for assistance, as defined by the Department of Environment (1989; 8-9), is determined by the housing authority on the basis of inquiries into previous accommodation, marital status, family circumstances, dependence, and income. A homeless person cannot make a recourse to a court in order to claim the right to housing.

Belgium: The law of 12 january 1993, known as the law Onkelinx, which constitutes the emergency programme for a greater social solidarity, may be considered as the legislation enabling access to general social assistance to homeless people. The law anticipated an inclusion in the communal laws of an article which authorizes the mayor to requisition buildings abandoned for more than six months and to transform them into dwellings for homeless people. The law also revoked the anti-vagrancy law and replaced the punitive measures against a homeless person by the dispositions obliging the welfare centres to provide social aid and access to the minimum subsistence means to homeless people. The responsibility of dealing with vagrants was thus revoked from the Department of Justice, and the competence to assist homeless people was assigned to the Community Ministers responsible for welfare and social affairs (Vranken and van Menxel, 1994).

1.3.2. Right to housing as a component of anti-poverty legislation

The most important direct financial transfers which guarantee access to the minimum living conditions to the socially excluded, are unemployment benefits and general non-contributory minimum income schemes and housing supplements. They are key instruments of the social legislation targeted at people entirely excluded from paid labour and who may never find a job, and those who were made redundant. Research undoubtedly shows that these two groups are at the highest risk of exclusion from adequate housing.

Unemployment schemes are established in the legislation of all Member States. The first laws based on the insurance schemes date back to the first half of the 20th century in Denmark (1907), the United Kingdom and Ireland (1911) Italy (1919), Luxembourg (1921), Belgium (1924), Germany (1927) and France (1940). Insurance and assistance schemes were introduced in the second part of the century in Greece (1954), Spain (1961), Portugal (1975) and the Netherlands (1986 as amended). The basic legislation which is currently in effect, is the outcome of a durable process of reaffirmation of principles and of legislative amendments.

To be eligible for unemployment benefits, in all Member States, claimants must be able and willing to work and be registered at the competent employment office (MISSOC, 1993). In principle, the entitlements are not means tested but the amount of unemployment benefit depends on the qualifying period. However, a ceiling for the amount of unemployment benefit that can be actually received is established in Belgium, Germany, Greece, Spain, France, Ireland (through pay-related insurance), Luxembourg, the Netherlands, and the United Kingdom. The duration of insurance based entitlements is generally limited and those who fall out of the safety net of unemployment entitlements may claim means-tested non-contributory entitlements, providing they are residents of a country or a region that has set up such schemes.

The subjective right and the non-discretionary entitlement to persons who have exhausted available possibilities of finding work, is founded in the basic national legislations of: Belgium (1974; 1976), Denmark (1974), Germany (1961), France (1988), Ireland (1975), Luxembourg (1986), the Netherlands (1963), and the United Kingdom (1987). Spain and Italy do not have uniform national laws, but respectively the Autonomous Communes and Regions are competent for the establishment of welfare benefits. Consequently, minimum income schemes are guaranteed only in some administrative units in Spain and Italy (For specific arrangements which vary according to different communes and regions see MISSOC, 1993; Tosi and Ranci, 1993; Salinas Ramos, 1993). Furthermore, in Spain only independent family units may be entitled to the allowance, as opposed to nine other European Union countries in which the right is universalistic and does not discriminate against individuals. Greece and Portugal have no general minimum income schemes.

The aim of non-contributory minimum income schemes is to protect from extreme poverty people who are not able to procure for themselves and their dependent family members sufficient resources to meet the basic needs. Under these schemes, financial assistance based on a statistical model of a hypothetical minimum subsistence level, or linked to the net minimum wage, or based on the guaranteed amount of old-age pensions, is transferred to the beneficiaries. Nationality is not a requirement for entitlement, but proof of residence in the country of the potentially eligible people is. Exceptions are German and Dutch nationals residing abroad who may also be granted social assistance. Illegally resident immigrants are not entitled to social welfare.

A housing supplement to the non-contributory benefit may be provided in Germany, France, Ireland, in some regions of Italy, Luxembourg, the Netherlands, and the United Kingdom. In Denmark housing component is taken into account and is part of the general allowance which is conceived to cover also the housing and related services (MISSOC, 1993). Although no specific reference is made to housing costs for establishing the amount of minimum income in Belgium, it must be acknowledged that the direct transfer in this country is based on a generous scheme. Indeed, the guaranteed amount of minimum subsistence means for a person living alone in Belgium in 1993 was the second highest in the European Union. The highest minimum income for persons living alone is in Luxembourg. A recent modification of the law on minimum guaranteed income (Law of 25 February 1993) has furthermore added a rent subsidy for beneficiaries of non-contributory benefits in Luxembourg.

Member States differ as to whether or not social transfers include specific benefits from which the poorest segments of the population can profit. But, they also differ considerably according to the share of the population receiving benefits and in the benefit levels. By way of example, unemployment benefits amount on the average to between 70 and 80 per cent of the GDP per head in Belgium, Denmark and the Netherlands. In Portugal and the United Kingdom they amount to 20 per cent, and in Italy and Greece only to 10 per cent of the GDP per head (Commission of the European Communities, 1993c). Access to benefits and levels of benefits are both indicators of rights and important variables of social and housing exclusion.

1.3.3. Right to housing as a component of housing legislation

Housing for the poor has traditionally been on the policy agenda since the early industrialization in the 19th century. The history of urban housing has typically been associated to:

> "... shortage, maladjustment of the offer to the demand, land speculation, marked inequality in the access to housing between social groups and according to localities, problems of maintenance of the housing stock, exceedingly high costs, problems of badly housed and homeless: all these symptoms have been manifesting over and over again for more than a century and are constituting grounds for policy action" (Lafore, 1993).[8]

---

[8] Translated from French by the author D. Avramov.

In order to meet the political challenge, governments have resorted to a variety of instruments to control the housing market. The wide spectre of measures included the regulation of construction standards, determination of obligations of owners and tenants, standardization of contractual terms of tenancy, control of rent levels, establishment of shared ownership, implementation of general schemes to facilitate access to home ownership, allocation of public resources into housing for low-earning groups, and tax reliefs for non-profit housing projects. In recent times, in order to maintain the solvency of the poor, rent and mortgage subsidies may be granted to individual low-income households.

While acknowledging the complexity of the housing legislation, social housing policies, and policy measures in diversified national contexts, a rigorous selection of most pertinent instruments is needed for the transnational overview. The analysis of implications of policy intervention in the domain of general and specific housing rights of all population sub-groups surpasses the scope of this report. We will focus only on the most relevant instruments of indirect and direct assistance to low-income and no-income groups. To illustrate the availability and affordability of housing for the poor in the Member States, we will focus on the most pertinent recent schemes of public investment into construction and renovation of housing for rent, and on forms of rent control. The question we will focus on is whether the homeless people can *de facto* access publicly subsidized housing for rent.

An attempt to identify the common denominator of policies determining systems of subsidies into bricks and into rents in the 12 European Union countries, inevitably does injustice to the complexity of national legislations, policies and social realities. The national context within which selected measures are developed and are being implemented is discussed in the Observatory's country reports for 1994 (Renard; Rostgaard and Koch Nielsen; Specht-Kittler; Salinas Ramos; de Gouy; Sapounakis; Tosi and Ranci; O'Sullivan; Wagner and Pels; de Feijter and Radstaak; Marques Balsa and Barreto; Carlisle) and can be consulted for specific reference.

1.3.3.1. Social housing: low-cost or market-conform housing?

In the first half of the century social housing was typically associated to the work related benefits. The construction of social housing was aimed at meeting the needs of blue collar and lower segments of white collar workers and alleviating the demographic pressure on cities. Social housing was typically located in suburban areas and contributed to the territorial concentration of groups of people with similar socio-economic background. From the 1960s onward, in some European Union countries access to non-contributory benefits and access to dwellings built and maintained with public resources was gradually being opened to people who are excluded from the paid labour.

Today, from the point of view of funding of social housing two basic types can be distinguished: social housing constructed and managed by the public organizations or by the non-profit organizations, and social housing constructed and maintained by private investors and housing associations (Commission of the European Communities, 1993b). The organizational set up may include three basic sections: cooperative, non-profit private and public section (CECODHAS, 1993).

The sector of social housing provides both dwellings for sale and for rent. Access to home ownership through social housing schemes is targeted at middle and lower-middle income groups and clearly does not address the needs of very low income groups and people outside the labour market. For people who are at risk of homelessness or are homeless, home ownership is entirely out of reach, even under the most generous social housing schemes. Social housing for letting at rent levels lower than free market rates, and rent rebate schemes for non-profit housing, address housing needs of low-earning households and those excluded from paid labour. The two groups which are at acute risk of being excluded from housing are dependent entirely on the rental sector of the housing market.

A brief history of access to social low-cost housing by the homeless and badly housed people is marked by numerous ambiguities. At the time when formal access to social housing was granted to those excluded from both labour and housing markets, European Union countries embarked on the process of disengagement of central authorities in the provision of low-cost housing, more particularly social housing for rent. The political orientation of the European Union countries is character-ized by a general tendency toward replacement of the statutory public sector provision of low-cost housing by the market-conform housing associations. The social housing constructed and maintained by the public sector is giving place to social housing constructed and maintained by private investors and housing enterprises. The process is marked by the decrease in the low-cost social housing stock, increased costs of social housing construction and growing rents. While policies of disengagement may be said to be converging at the Union level, the legislative options and the commitment of resources to bridge the gap between the housing market and housing exclusion are by no means uniform.

Access to social housing subsidized by the public sector is generally means-tested, exceptions are Denmark and the United Kingdom. This implies that income thresholds delimit access to publicly funded housing only to the lower income segments of the population in the majority of European Union countries. The question which we will address in this section is whether the lowest income segment of the population, and more particularly the homeless people can actually claim access to publicly funded housing and, if not, to what degree the condition of homelessness may be an obstacle to access to subsidized housing. The key issue addressed in this section is the extent to which access to publicly funded housing is equitable.

Access to housing by the homeless and people at risk of becoming homeless may be said to be in principle an enforceable right in France and in the United Kingdom. The first has established in its legislative system the right to housing for all, the second has introduced statutory measures of preferential access to housing for groups who cannot compete on the formal housing market due to their income insufficiency or other handicaps.

In the remaining 10 European Union countries access by homeless and people threatened by homelessness to subsidized housing is not an enforceable claim. The social aspect of public housing is maintained through the allocation system which operates by means of income thresholds and rent rebates for low-income households. The formal definition of priorities and target groups does not differ substantially between countries. What, however, does differ is the extent of accompanying measures of social policy and the actual transfer of resources to the most needy segment of the population. The practical implication is that in the process of implementation of criteria for the allocation of social housing, the social condition of homelessness may give people priority, may be taken into account, or may *a priori* exclude them from access to publicly funded or state subsidised housing.

In Belgium, Germany, Ireland and Luxembourg the provision of low-cost subsidized housing for rent is established in the country's legislation and people receiving non-contributory or unemployment benefits are eligible for social housing and may also be entitled to housing benefits and rent rebates. Denmark and the Netherlands focus to a lesser degree on the formal recognition of the right. But, through their social practice, the two countries implement generous transfers to households in order to overcome their income insufficiency and enable them to adjust to market-conform mechanisms under which social housing operates. In Spain, Greece, Portugal and to a lesser degree in Italy, absence of general non-contributory entitlements implies that access to social housing is *de facto* tied to the employment record. Under a system of points and income guarantees public housing administration may decline access to housing to homeless people who have no income and no abode. Homeless people who are excluded from regular paid labour cannot exhibit proof that they will be able to pay rents regularly. The complexity of criteria for the allocation of social housing in Italy implies that there are important elements in the general points system for "catching" situations of housing exclusion. But, in a situation of severe shortage of affordable housing, they do not assure coverage for all the most needy groups (Tosi and Ranci, 1994).

In addition to the shortage in the supply of social housing, the condition which the group of southern countries share with many other Member States, the lack of comprehensive social policy which would be founded in the domestic legislation is the principal impediment to the access to the welfare provisions and publicly funded housing by the homeless people. Legislation and public policies make no effective commitment to provide permanent housing to non-earning groups.

1.3.3.1.1. Statutory access to social housing

In France and the United Kingdom homeless and potentially homeless people are eligible for social housing and legal instruments have been introduced to provide statutory access to housing. The local authorities have an obligation to monitor housing needs of vulnerable groups and to allocate financial means and provide urgent accommodation and housing for no-income and low-income people.

France: In the French social housing system the public sector and private non-profit housing organizations provide low-cost housing by supplying rental units and access to home ownership for low-income groups. Public aid is allocated for construction, renovation, maintenance and management of low-rent housing, fiscal exemptions, and aids to certain categories of tenants. Non-profit housing associations which operate within the social housing system must be social vocation units, and have to apply regulated rents and resource ceilings for the tenants they house. They are obliged to undergo government audits (Devlin, 1994). Local and regional authorities have to contribute to the financial input of the central authorities.

The Law for the Orientations of Cities and Towns (Loi d'orientation sur la ville, 1991) introduced qualitative changes in the global system of housing subventions and imposed financial solidarity between communes. Namely, one part of the state subsidies is directed from more prosperous to less developed communes which usually have greater needs for social housing. The law recommends that the state and the local communities coordinate action for the development of local housing programmes. If such programmes are not elaborated, the prefect is authorized to modify urban planning documents in communes in which social housing accounts for less than 20 percent of the total housing stock to ensure that it becomes available. The law promotes the concept of diversification of housing with integration of social dwellings in the urban texture so as to avoid housing segregation of low-income groups.

In order to accomplish the housing policy aims by putting in place dispositions for the implementation of the right to housing, another legislative act, the law 94-624, was recently passed (Law of 21 July 1994). The law imposed legal obligations on the local authorities to provide urgent assistance to homeless people and those threatened by homelessness. The law committed departments to elaborating a plan for urgent accommodation of homeless and low-income people by 31 December 1994. Communes with 10,000 to 100,000 inhabitants are obliged to provide one place for the homeless per 2,000 of its inhabitants, and communes with more than 100,000 inhabitants, one emergency accommodation place for every 1,000 inhabitants.

This may be considered as an interim measure that puts in place a programme to bridge the gap between no shelter and permanent accommodation. The obligation to ensure that sufficient temporary shelter is available should be seen as a step forward in the process of ensuring proper housing (de Gouy, 1994).

United Kingdom: In England, the Housing Act (1988) assigned to the local authorities an enabling, rather than statutory role and emphasized private finance for social housing. The 1988 Act marked the shift towards market rents and decreased security of tenure of many households in social housing. Housing Associations have become the main providers of newly-built social housing whilst the local authority has nomination rights to a predetermined share of dwellings. Typically, three quarters of new housing is allocated to people nominated by the local authority (Carlisle, 1994).

Local authorities have a duty to keep a record of people who need accommodation and to determine, together with housing associations, how local housing is to be allocated. The waiting list is formed on the basis of the allocation policy of the local community. However, under the statutory requirement of the Housing Act (1985, Section 22) reasonable preference in the allocation of public housing is recommended for people in priority need.

The Local Government and Housing Act (1989) abolished the obligation for local authorities to keep a housing stock. The Act focused on issues of quality and safety of rented dwellings rather than on how to access housing. It introduced new criteria of fitness for human habitation for all dwellings, those belonging to housing associations and private sector landlords, as well as for public housing. It foresees that the local authority can take action against a landlord if a dwelling becomes unfit. The 1989 Act introduced a new system of renovation grants which are means-tested on income levels and financial resources.

Under the 1988 Housing Order of Northern Ireland, the Housing Executive has the duty to provide housing for people who are unintentionally homeless and in priority need. In 1994 the Northern Ireland Housing Executive published a draft housing strategy for the 1995-1998 period. Four areas of activity are identified: social home building, reinvestment programme into existing dwellings, maintenance programme to preserve good standards of quality of social housing, and public investment into private homes in order to improve housing conditions.

In Scotland the Housing Act (1987) determines conditions for the allocation of local authority housing. Local authorities are obliged to establish housing waiting lists and publish rules about how houses are allocated. In allocating housing, local authorities must give reasonable preference to people living in substandard housing, overcrowded dwellings, large families, those living under precarious conditions, and people who are homeless. Housing associations providing social rented housing are not bound by the clause on priorities mentioned in the Act. However, most have nomination agreements with local authorities that 50 per cent of dwellings are rented to nominees from the local authority (Aldridge, 1994).

1.3.3.1.2. Preferential access to low-cost and market-conform social housing

Criteria defining preferential access to low-cost and market-conform housing are part of the enabling provisions which define responsibilities of authorities, but are not sufficiently strong to require authorities to house the homeless. In Belgium, Denmark, Germany, Ireland, Luxembourg and the Netherlands the provision of low-cost subsidized housing for rent is established in the countries legislation or in the social practice. The legal framework in Belgium and in Germany is characterized by a limited legislative role of the central government which remains largely empowering in its nature. The establishment of the right is under the competence of regions and local authorities. Denmark and the Netherlands focus to a lesser degree on enabling legislation and are committed rather to policy measures which facilitate access to housing for the homeless people. The six countries, Belgium, Denmark, Germany, Ireland, Luxembourg and the Netherlands, have foreseen instruments for preferential access to social housing for homeless people. However, they have not established instruments which would entitle a homeless person to claim the right to a home.

Belgium: The introduction of the right to housing clause in the new Belgian Constitution (1994) marks an advance stage in the process of the legislative establishment of social rights as citizen's rights. The task of providing instruments and allocating resources for the application of the existing legislation, passing new laws and setting up channels through which individuals could claim the right to housing, is still being negotiated. The legislation currently in vigour includes a number of relevant empowering instruments for dealing with homelessness.

Throughout the 1980s and 1990s access to housing has not been entirely left to spontaneous market mechanisms. Relative Housing Acts of Wallonia, Flanders and Brussels-Capital define the public policy aims of rigorous management of the housing stock in order to increase the offer (Fierens, 1993). Access to property and access to rented housing includes complex schemes of subsidies in all three Belgian regions. Incentives provided by the public authorities for housing include provisions for construction by the social housing associations of housing blocks for rent in less prosperous localities (Flanders, 1991; Wallonia, 1992). Public authorities subvention local authorities to finance the infrastructure in social housing allotments.

The law of 4 August 1992 which regulates mortgage loans has imposed limits on the variation in interest rates. Loans at preferential interest rates are guaranteed by the state, by public social housing associations, regional funds for housing large families, general savings and pension bond, and authorized agencies. Numerous tax reliefs are implemented including a preferential V.A.T. on social housing and for housing for the handicapped and persons in difficulty.

A multitude of regulations adopted at the level of local communities pertain to standards of adequacy of housing and clearance of slum areas and renovation of insalubrious dwellings. There is no national or regional standardized definition of insalubrious dwelling but there is a well defined general orientation. In accordance with Article 67 of the Housing Act, the mayor of a commune can order execution of works of renovation or demolition of insalubrious housing. Before declaring a housing unit insalubrious, the mayor is obliged to make sure that sufficient low-cost social housing is made available for rehousing the tenants. Subventions for demolition or renovation of insalubrious dwellings are provided by the public authorities to social housing associations or to communes. A special subvention is anticipated for the renovation of insalubrious dwellings for housing homeless and badly housed people (1988).

The law Onkelinx (1993), as mentioned before, has a housing component which enables the requisition of abandoned buildings and their transformation by the local authorities into dwellings for homeless people.

The Housing Act empowers the regional housing authorities to appoint social housing associations to build moderate cost housing for rent. Those housing associations benefit from long-term loans for the duration of 66 years, and from other financial and fiscal benefits. Allocation of low cost social housing is made in accordance with standards developed and adopted at the communal level. They are targeted at people without a personal dwelling, people in bad housing, and people who are in difficulty due to household changes. Typically, the majority of applicants are beneficiaries of the minimum non-contributory benefit, unemployment benefit or retirement pension. Although private investors may be entirely responsible for social housing funding, its social protection of low-income groups is maintained by the rent adjustment according to income.

Public welfare care centres (in Dutch O.C.M.W; in French C.P.A.S.) may have a role in providing social housing by engaging, alone or with housing associations, in building and renovating housing for aged, handicapped or other persons who cannot provide for their own housing (Law of 8 July 1976). They can also cover rent costs for large families or those in difficulty.

Denmark: Construction policies aim to increase the quantity and improve the quality of the housing stock and to create new jobs. Housing policies address individual households and their economic and social needs (Rostgaard and Koch-Nielsen, 1994).

Social housing in Denmark was not conceived to provide housing for special categories or low-income groups. There is no income threshold and social housing is accessible to all. Its aim is to provide good quality dwellings at a reasonable price to all, and to achieve a mixed composition of tenants. Social goals are achieved through rent rebate, interest rate subsidies and housing allowances. A definition of the social housing would accordingly include all rental dwellings subject to regulation and/or subsidisation, non-profit housing, co-operative housing and housing for the elderly and the young (Commission of the European Communities, 1993b). The general welfare assistance includes the rent rebate for tenants and tax reliefs for owner occupied dwellings.

Although social housing is made available to all, a number of facilitating instruments are set in place for low-income groups and people with social problems. Non-profit housing associations are the main service providers for these groups and they operate under the Act of Housing Construction. The associations are in charge of the construction and management of the non-profit rental housing. The entire financing of construction is provided by funds external to the housing association (Commission of the European Communities, 1993b). Between 80 and 96 per cent of construction costs are covered by an indexed loan guaranteed by the government. A capital subsidy of between 4 and 13 per cent is provided by the local authorities and the tenant's deposit ranges from 2 to 20 per cent of the costs.

The non-profit housing sector operated under a system of national quotas until 1 January 1994. Since then, the quota system has been decentralized and local authorities are designated to establish needs. Access to non-profit housing may be granted via regular waiting lists. Applicants have to be over 15 years of age and pay a deposit every year. Dwellings are allocated according to the size of the household and presence of children gives preferential access to large apartments. Allocation by local authorities is made when applicants are in acute need of a dwelling. For this purpose, local authorities may claim one fourth or more of the non-profit housing stock. They take up the payment of rent from the moment of allocation until the applicant moves into a dwelling. Allocation according to special social criteria addresses the housing needs of divorcees, low-income households, physically handicapped and elderly people. Homeless or socially-excluded persons may be housed under these provisions, and it is up to the non-profit housing association to decide on introduced requests. The association is not permitted to make inquiries about the applicant, and they do not have an obligation to make public the number of applicants who gain access to housing on the basis of special social criteria (Rostgaard and Koch-Nielsen, 1994).

The newly-built social housing is often more expensive than old, privately rented dwellings. In Greater Copenhagen the rent per square meter in privately owned rental housing is 40 per cent cheaper than in the new non-profit housing. In the Danish welfare system the rent rebate secures equitable housing conditions for different income groups rather than the provision of low-cost housing.

Germany: The communal laws set minimum standards for the provision of housing. They define the scope of indirect claims to accommodation and provide a degree of security to tenants faced with the prospect of loosing a dwelling (Specht-Kittler, 1993). Each of the 16 Lander has its Regulatory Authority Acts, but typically they are committed to providing communal emergency shelter and to allocating the potentially homeless person his own dwelling or sequestrating another private dwelling and allocating it to the homeless person. A homeless person is assumed to be a "disturber" of public security and thus assistance is seen as a measure to protect public interests. Accommodation provided under the communal law is a transitory measure, and the length of time for which housing is provided does not exceed six months.

The Controlled Tenancies Act, which defines terms of access to council homes, the Housing and Rent Law and the Public Welfare Law define a comprehensive system of the right to housing. The most important legal provisions are contained in the Federal Public Welfare Act in the chapter (11-26 BSHG) dealing with assistance to the needy. The housing provisions are defined under Help for Special Cases clause (72 BSHG). The taking-over of the costs of accommodation and of debts is defined in sections 12 and 15 of the Act, while needs of groups already homeless are addressed in section 72. The Controlled Tenancies Act regulates the allocation procedures while the housing agencies of the communes and districts reserve allocation rights for a limited number of publicly subsidised dwellings. Typically, the housing agency proposes three applicants of whom the landlord chooses one. A prerequisite for access to low-cost housing is a possession of a certificate which confirms an entitlement to accommodation in a council/corporation home. Under the Housing Law, income thresholds and household size are the only legal requirement for eligibility to the entitlement. They are the core of the social priority criteria for allocation of low-cost housing which are defined at the Federal level. Pregnancy of a woman may facilitate access to social housing of low-income groups.

Ireland: The aim of social housing is to ensure that every family can live in a dwelling of good quality which can be purchased or rented at an affordable price in an acceptable environment. This aim is to be pursued "as far as the resources of the economy permit" (Plan for Social Housing, 1992). The legislative framework for housing provision, part of their funding, development of general policies and monitoring of implementation is provided by the Department of Environment. The responsibility for the delivery of services is on the local housing authority. The Plan for Social Housing is one of the instruments of the Housing Act which, as mentioned before, transfers the responsibility for monitoring homelessness and assessing the housing needs to the local authorities, but does not impose a requirement to do so.

As of 1992 the housing authorities are asked to examine the option of purchasing existing houses, rather than building large estates of new dwellings. The aim of the policy is to promote smaller, well designed schemes with a more intimate environment, and integrated as far as possible with other housing so as to prevent social segregation in housing (O'Sullivan, 1994).

The Plan for Social Housing envisages a wider approach than just building or baying dwellings for rent. In order to speed up access to housing:

> "Local authorities will need to explain the various housing options now available to persons on their waiting lists, give them all relevant information, and provide advice appropriate to the individual circumstances. Generally, the measures in this plan rate on equal basis new built and refurbishment of existing buildings. Local authorities will be urged to regard to the advantages of renewing older buildings, redeveloping older areas and using existing infrastructure in pursuing their housing policies." (Department of Environment, 1991, p. 34)

Luxembourg: The establishment of the Fund for moderate cost housing (Fonds pour le logement à coût modéré) marks an important step towards a comprehensive social housing policy in Luxembourg (Law of 25 February 1979). The Fund aims at providing means for the acquisition of land and construction of low cost housing for sale or for rent. It is targeted at meeting the urgent needs for accommodation within the framework of a policy of friendly housing environment and integration of new social housing in the existing structures. The law anticipates direct subventions for the construction and renovation which are targeted at low-income groups. The subventions may be directly allocated for the construction or may be transferred through subsidizing interest payments for housing loans. In order to meet the needs of low income groups which cannot purchase even a low-cost subsidized dwelling, the Fund provides housing for rent. The rent levels are adjusted according to the income of tenants. The Fund also administers social housing.

The Netherlands: Three forms of subsidies operate: dwelling-related subsidies, land or location-tied subsidies and individual rent subsidies. The Social and Cultural Planning Agency of the Government in its 1994 report advised the government to negotiate with the housing associations provisions to make sufficient low-cost housing available. The elaboration of special arrangements is seen as necessary because the decentralization policy has limited the role of the central government and cut-backs in government subsidies have resulted in marked rent increases (de Feijter and Radstaak, 1994). Social housing associations still have an obligation to provide housing for low-income groups, but since they have to operate under market conditions, social housing has generally ceased to be low-cost housing. The subsidy for social rented housing is provided in the form of annual contributions to the landlord and the individual rent subsidy is an option for low-income groups. These direct transfers to low-income groups are devised as the principal instrument to bridge the gap between income insufficiency and the housing market. The model of low-cost social housing is gradually being substituted by rent subsidies for low-income households. These subsidies, together with other social benefits provided to broad categories of citizens for unlimited duration are supposed to enable fulfilment of basic needs including adequate housing.

1.3.3.1.3. Low-priority access for homeless people to subsidized housing

Greece: The right to housing in Greece falls in the broad category of non-enforceable social rights which were introduced in the programme part of the constitution of 1975. Statutory measures are foreseen in order to assist people without any, or with inadequate, accommodation (Article 21 paragraphs 3 and 4), but are not specifically elaborated in the constitution or in other legal instruments.

There is little direct public investment in funding social housing and the available assistance is largely aimed at ownership (Commission of the European Communities, 1993b).

The Organization for Worker's Housing (OEK) is the principal authority responsible for the construction, allocation and administration of social housing. The Organization is subsidised by the government. The prerequisites for eligibility for social housing are employment in a private or public enterprise which is insured by the public social security fund, and payment of an income-related contribution of one percent to the Organization. Minimum insured days of work for eligibility for Organization for Worker's Housing scheme vary according to the family size and social and physical handicaps (See: Sapounakis, 1994). Income thresholds constitute the main criteria of eligibility for the work-related social housing scheme. Blue collar and low earning white collar workers are typical beneficiaries of social housing.

The Welfare Department of the Ministry of Health, Welfare and Social Security provides housing under a complex set of rules. Three categories are being assisted; repatriated persons and refugees who are eligible for housing benefits, households stricken by natural disaster and low-income households. The so-called Popular Housing for low-income households is not funded through an insurance scheme but is state financed. However, in its limited scope it remains largely a work-related assistance to low-paid categories.

Italy: The major social intervention operates through the public housing construction schemes (Edilizia Residenziale Pubblica - EPR) which include construction by the state or provision by the state of financial support for construction. Although social housing policies are currently being redefined they are still strongly centred on construction and characterized by a decentralized system of responsibility between the central, regional and local government.

The subsidized housing scheme is a direct intervention by the state which covers the entire costs of construction and remains the owner of property which is in turn rented to low-income families. Under the scheme, funding is provided to local governments for the renovation of the housing stock or to the local housing authorities for the construction of new dwellings and for the renovation of the public housing stock. The obligatory contribution introduced in 1949 and amended in 1963 is made by companies and is deduced from wages. The funds are pooled into the Committee for Residential Building and subsequently distributed to regions. The income ceiling for access to subsidized social housing is determined by regions, and the rent is adjusted to the income level of tenants.

The facilitating housing scheme builds on the financial support to housing projects using bank loans to build dwellings which can be sold or rented. Under this scheme the state pays all or part of the bank interest on 15 year loans. The finance is provided directly by the central government for projects which meet preset financial and technical criteria (Tosi and Ranci, 1994). Applicants may range from local social housing authorities, local authorities, shared ownership schemes, cooperatives, public agencies, construction companies, to private individuals constructing or renovating a dwelling for the first occupancy. Income thresholds are the discriminatory criteria for eligibility and three different income bands are foreseen.

The basic requirements for assignment of social housing are income ceilings, citizenship, and registration as resident, or having a job, within the local community. Priorities are defined on the basis of a certain number of criteria: family income, family type (young couples, families with handicapped persons, large families, families with elderly persons, etc;) housing conditions (amenities, overcrowding, "improper housing", etc). Priority may be given to households threatened by eviction. Quotas of social housing have been reserved, under the pressure of emergency legislation, to specific groups and urban areas. However, the homeless and very poor people may be unfavoured by the points system and may depend only on the discretionary intervention of the social assistance system (Tosi and Ranci, 1994).

The institutional system does not guarantee an enforceable right to housing and there are no consistent or effective guarantees of priority for the homeless either. The efficacy of the institutional provision is largely dependent on the amount of resources invested in social housing. The Italian model of distribution of responsibilities between the central state and regions grants high discretionary powers to local authorities. The type and extent of housing assistance actually provided derives from a multitude of policy choices made at the level of regions which have planning and legislative competence, and on administrative options decided by the communes which are empowered for local administration. The final outcome is the differential treatment of groups in housing needs according to regions and communes. Moreover, the complex system of criteria and procedures for accessing social housing, in a situation of severe shortage of affordable supply, does not assure coverage for all the most needy groups, nor priority for the homeless (Tosi and Ranci, 1994)

Portugal: The promotion of social housing introduced in Portugal as early as 1918 was abandoned in 1982 as a direct state intervention (Marques Balsa and Barreto, 1994). The extinction of the Fund for Housing Development (Fundo de Fomento da Habitacao) in 1982 marks the disengagement of the state and the transfer of the public housing initiative to the local administration. The indirect state intervention is, however, maintained through the provision of housing subsidies for low-cost housing construction, subsidies for payments of interest rates on housing loans, preferential interest rates for specific categories of (young) households or saving accounts earmarked for housing, and fiscal measures. Furthermore, the state has maintained a role in negotiating with local administration programmes to renovate degraded quarters and to rehouse their residents.

Public financial intervention is mainly targeted at promoting access to property by granting loans at reduced rates, and fiscal benefits. The Institute for Alienation of the State Housing Stock (IGAPHE) provides the financing and the maintenance of social rental dwellings and encourages the sale to tenants. Access to rental social housing and publicly subsidized home ownership is determined by the average levels of monthly income of the family. It corresponds to one minimum national wage for the rental sector, and three minimal national wages for the purchase of controlled-cost housing units (Commission of the European Communities, 1993b).

The Revision of the Urban Rental System, after rents were unfrozen in 1985, allowed for the signing of term contracts, creation of a scheme of tax incentives to rental, both for the landlord and the tenant, exemption from municipal tax, up to 10 years, for dwellings intended for lease, and creation of a rent subsidy for young people.

Spain: The government's Housing plan 1992-1995 specifies the general policy orientation. Namely, the plan gives preference to ownership subventions over subsidies to the rental sector, and it determines conditions of eligibility. It may be said that the housing policy has been mainly associated to fiscal measures, as approximately 70 percent of state subsidies for housing are allocated to the payment of interest rates on loans. In terms of allocation of public resources, home-ownership is given priority over social housing for rent (Salinas Ramos, 1994). Financing for the purchase of dwellings includes an elaborate system of requirements and fiscal measures (See: Commission of the European Communities, 1993b). Officially protected social housing is funded by the Autonomous Regions and its development by the public sector only included dwellings for rent in very special cases. The central government invests only in dwellings of public promotion and of general interest.

Under the Housing Plan, conditions of eligibility for publicly pooled resources include a minimum income threshold. Applicants for the officially protected housing of public promotion for rent or sale, must not exceed the familiar weighed income of 2.5 times the minimum inter-professional wage. Officially protected housing of general schemes is targeted at the population with higher weighed family incomes which, however, must not exceed 5.5 times the minimum inter-professional wage. In fixing the rents of social housing terms are different for the first income threshold group and are fixed by the basis law and by the specific terms of the Autonomous Communities. These rents may be subject to subsidization. For the second threshold group the very highest rent levels are fixed by administrative terms.

Within the framework of urban planning, administration can undertake clearance of city quarters. If expropriation measures are applied in order to pursue public construction works, the authorities are obliged to provide public housing units to rehouse affected households. People living in sub-standard housing can thus be allocated publicly funded housing. But, this provision results from authorities' urban planning projects which affect particular districts rather than from projects to house the target social groups.

Since the provision of publicly funded social housing is within the competence of the autonomous communes, the extent of intervention varies from one administrative unit to another, as well do rent levels which may be fixed according to specific regional terms.

1.3.3.2. Rent rebate or rent control : solvency or affordability?

A multitude of systems of indirect and direct rent control and rent rebate may be traced in the European Union countries. Where there are no rent ceilings for the private rented sector, tenants may be legally protected from rent increases during the validity of the tenancy agreement. Frequently, a system of annual rent indexation is set up. Public housing for rent has traditionally been the sector to which schemes of rent control have been applied. In recent years, however, social housing has become increasingly more expensive and (quasi) market social housing associations are becoming principal providers of new rental units. Housing authorities in the United Kingdom, Ireland, the Netherlands and Italy have resorted to a massive sale of housing built with public funds. The current policy orientation builds on a model of market-conform social housing with market rents. The social character of the housing policy is expected to be maintained through individualized rent subsidy schemes and direct transfers to targeted households. Thus, the focus is not on keeping rents low, but on maintaining the solvency of the poor through direct financial transfers to households.

Denmark may be considered as the forerunner in the housing allowance and benefit schemes and provides an example of the model of direct intervention aimed at individual households. The tax reform introduced in 1993 (Boligministeriet, 1993) provided financial benefits for the owner-occupied housing, while the rent rebate addressed assistance to tenants. The scheme consists of the housing allowance, 75 per cent of which is subsidized by the state and 25 per cent by the municipality, and of the housing benefit 40 per cent of which is subsidized by the state and 60 per cent by the municipality. The first is restricted to pensioners regardless of whether or not they are living in non-profit housing, co-operatives or owner-occupied dwellings. The second is allocated to low-income groups in rented dwellings. There is an upper limit on the rebate both for the allowance and for the benefit. The rebate covers the difference between the minimum amount paid by the beneficiary and the actual cost of rent. The rent rebate schemes are set up to provide access to the housing market by transferring financial assistance directly to individuals so that they can pay rents which they would not otherwise be able to afford.

Belgium, Germany, France, Ireland, Luxembourg, the Netherlands and the United Kingdom are, to different degrees, also moving away from the model of low-cost social housing. It remains to be seen whether the replacement of low-cost social housing by market-conform housing will be complemented by a sufficient housing supply and by comprehensive direct financial transfers to low-income households which cannot compete on the housing market. In Chapter 3 we will address the issue of quantity, quality and affordability of the housing stock in the 1990s.

Here it may suffice to stress that the control of rent levels has been largely eroded over recent years and that rent and mortgage subsidies, even in their limited scope, are being reviewed.

Against the social and economic background which prevailed in the group of southern European Member States; Italy, Portugal and Greece, the control of rent levels operated as a major social corrective. The model used in these countries was that of rent freeze and rent control, rather than of non-contributory benefits targeted at individual households. In Spain where private ownership was given preferential access to public resources, relevant financial resources were neither allocated to the social rental sector, nor was the rental sector operating under rent control conditions.

When market conditions threatened social structures, Italy and Portugal resorted to rent freezes. This did not require considerable allocation of publicly pooled resources and their redistribution to target groups, but the measure constituted a *de facto* redistribution of resources between owners and tenants. In order to establish more just contractual tenancy terms for owners, rent control mechanisms substituted rent freeze. In more recent years, liberalization of rents marks a turning point in the housing policy.

After decades of rent freeze in Italy, the Fair Rent Act (Law No. 392) was passed in 1978 in order to implement the criteria for the establishment of rent levels, indexed rent increase, the duration of contracts and procedures of repossession. The law established parameters for determining rent levels according to the location, size and age, state of repair, accessory facilities, and determined the rent indexation system. Owners were, in return, guaranteed the right to evict tenants and to give them advance notice. Under conditions of acute shortage of low-cost housing, one of the ambiguous consequences of the legislative change was almost one million eviction procedures processed by courts between 1983 and 1991 (Tosi and Ranci, 1994). The system of rent control *de facto* ended in 1992 when the Law No. 359/92 liberalized the rental market by opening the possibility for the stipulation of rental agreements outside the limits set in the Fair Rent Act.

Under the Portuguese rent control legislation, rents were blocked between 1948 and 1985. The Civil Code (1966) guaranteed permanency of family tenure by extending to surviving family members the tenure rights. Adoption of the Law 46/85 and supplements DL 13/86 and Portaria 227/86, mark the beginning of the process of rent liberalization. The process of de-regularization was completed in 1990 by the DL 321-B/90 Act which defines the terms of urban rent regime (Régime de Arrendamento Urbano). The measures allow the revision of rents and open the door to complete liberalization of the rental sector (Marques Balsa and Barreto, 1994). Owners are the beneficiaries of legislative changes which enable free establishment of rents, stipulation of limited duration tenure and limited access to tenure of the descendent of the household head.

Protected rent schemes are reserved only for dwellings rented prior to 1985. Old tenants benefit from automatic renewal of tenure and indexed rents. Since the rent for the base year to which indexation is applied is very low, despite the annual increase, rents remain at levels far below the current market-determined rents. This measure has protected mainly the older segment of the population.

The practice of rent control was introduced in Greece in the post-Second World War period to counterbalance the housing shortage. The law No. 709/87, currently in effect, has similar aims. The protection of tenants has, however, not been fully effective. Regardless of the rent regulation, rents increased by 30 per cent between 1986 and 1988 (Depos, 1990), and the informal market evolved parallel to the administered one. "In the market the ratio between the real and the "administered rent" is usually two to one" (Sapounakis, 1994). The policy of progressive de-regularization of the rented housing sector is based on the law No. 709/87 which established terms for the segmentation of the stock according to the size of dwellings. The threshold of 120 square meters, later lowered to 90 square meters, marks the line between controlled and liberalized rents. Namely owners of dwelling below the threshold size have to comply with administered rent raises.

1.4. PROVISION OF MEANS

The process of establishment of the right to housing does not end with the passing of laws. It does not suffice to know that one may have a just claim to a non-enforceable right to a home. It may mean little to know that one may have a just claim to a home when authorities have a high discretionary power in interpreting targets and entitlements. The formal and procedural obstacles which people may encounter realizing the right to a home have one common denominator: insufficient provision of means. Indeed, the provision of means to access the proclaimed rights is the key measure of the political and juridical commitment to the realization of the right to housing.

The illustration of the degree to which the allocation of resources may be (in)appropriate and (not)well targeted at the needy, may be interpreted in the broader context of the background factors of housing exclusion. Indeed, those issues will be addressed in Chapter 3. However, injustice would be done to homeless and badly housed people if too much credit was given to the formal commitment of governments and their planned initiatives which may derive from the legal framework. Indeed, governments may reluctantly adopt policy measures and pass laws under high political pressure, but undermine the commitment by inadequate allocation of resources. Therefore, we believe that basic information which documents the rift between political intentions, legal commitments and the actual allocation of resources is needed to highlight the process of establishment of the right to housing.

The policy and legal commitment is made effective by the allocation of overall social resources, and cannot be reduced merely to the financial input. However, allocation of financial resources remains the critical measure of a country's commitment to defend the inherent dignity of a homeless person. Governments have pledged to prevent homelessness and to assist people excluded from housing. But, homeless and potentially homeless people are just one of many target groups of social policy. Indeed, governments have the competence to establish social priorities and target groups of social protection and to allocate the country's maximum available resources for national social security. Thus, the actual provision of means for no-income and low-income people needs to be measured against the broad background of social protection. What is the actual "weight" of the government's commitment to minimum standards of decent living? How much of the country's financial resources are allocated to low-income and no-income people who are at risk of being excluded from housing or have already lost their home?

The prevailing social policy system is an expression of long negotiated terms of social and intergenerational solidarity. The social protection addresses risks associated with ageing, sickness and income loss. The overall volume of resources allocated for social protection may be said to be a compromise between desirability and affordability. Currently, in the European Union the social protection budget accounts for almost one quarter of the gross domestic product, and covers virtually the whole population. When risks of income loss materialize due to sickness, retirement and unemployment a broad range of income protection schemes and transfers to restore income losses enter into effect.

The redistribution of allocated resources by groups of functions reflects the putting into operation of relative priority schemes within the national social protection system. The magnitude of social transfers to people excluded from the labour force and dependent on non-contributory benefits and housing benefits for their minimum subsistence means needs to be perceived as part of the provision of means for the entire system of social protection.

Social protection priorities are reflected in the allocation of resources to targeted population sub-groups and to targeted domains of protection. According to the group of functions, the highest share is allocated to old age survivors, followed by health, family-maternity and employment-unemployment. Between 1980 and 1989 the share of old age-survivors grouping increased from 43.7 per cent to 45.9 per cent. Over the same period, for the Union as a whole, health grouping fell from 37.6 per cent to 36.2 per cent. Family-maternity benefits increased from 7.9 per cent to 10.4 per cent. Resources allocated for unemployment and promotion of employment increased marginally from 6.3 per cent to 6.6 per cent, but trends diverged considerably between countries. Social protection benefits allocated to housing grouped together with other or miscellaneous functions under EUROSTAT's classification, clearly show that housing and assisting the poor is placed at the bottom of the priority list in terms of allocation of public resources (Graph 1).

The broad variety of social protection benefits include health care, sickness-cash benefits, maternity, invalidity, old age, survivors, employment injuries and occupational diseases, family benefits, unemployment and specific non-contributory minima. The non-contributory minima are generally the lowest guaranteed household income.

In order to measure the total cost of the scheme, more complete data than those currently made available are necessary. However, the overview of the situation on July 1st 1993 published by the Commission of the European Communities may be used as the basis for an estimation. The total costs of general non-contributory minima, aimed at protecting adults in the working age group excluded from the labour market and their dependent family members who have no other entitlements, can be tentatively assessed at around 8.5 billion ECU. The entitlement was transferred to some 10,6 million people, in the working age and able and willing to work, but who had no access to paid labour or to any income (Estimated on basis of data in: MISSOC, 1993). This figure does not include old age, invalidity, and other specific non-contributory minima. When compared to the total budget for social protection, which in 1989 stood at ECU 1,168 Billion (EUROSTAT, 1991) it remains clear that the general minimum subsistence means allocated to the poorest segment of the population account for a small fraction of total social protection spending. Less than one percent of the social protection spending was targeted specifically at three percent of the total population of the Member States who would have lived in absolute poverty had they not received the general minimum subsistence means.

Graph 1: Social protection benefits by groups of functions: proportion of total benefits

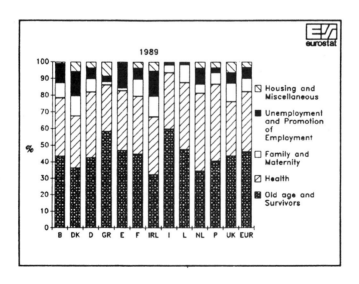

Source: EUROSTAT, 1991

Even the report of the 5th meeting of the European Ministers of Housing did not come up with the approximative figure for public social rented housing financing. It limited its finding to the statement about diversity of types of funding and methods used to set it up (Commission of the European Communities, 1993b). The share of the budget dedicated to housing and miscellaneous benefits, as seen in Graph 1, is small in comparison to other functions covered by social protection. Housing function which covers payments made on behalf of certain categories of households accounted on the average for 1.8 per cent of the overall social benefits in 1991 (Commission of the European Communities, 1993c). The portion allocated to subvention of low-cost dwellings for rent and for rent subventions and rent rebates for the poorest segment of the population, constitutes only a small fraction of public social housing funding.

In terms of allocation of public resources, housing the poor and homeless in Europe today, and maintaining the solvency of the poor, consumes a small portion of national social security budgets. This is generally not made clear to the general public when policy discussions take place on sustainability of social protection costs and when cost contingency proposals are made by the authorities. An evaluation of the economic impact of savings which may result from the public disengagement in the provision of low-cost social housing for rent, and of the extent of budgetary gains that would be made if minimum subsistence schemes and housing benefits for non-earning groups were dismantled, would require an in-depth economic analysis which goes far beyond the scope of this report. However, one can express serious doubts as to the gains that the population as a whole might have if cuts in subsidies to the poorest segment of the population were made. By contrast, it would not require as much effort to document the disastrous effect on the poor and homeless themselves and on the entire system of social solidarity.

Under conditions of structurally induced long-term unemployment, pressures by different social forces are increasing to revise the concept of social risks on which the European model of social security is founded. The direction in which the provision of means will evolve, depends largely on whether the risk of income loss will be perceived as accidental and temporary, or as a permanent condition which fragilizes particular population sub-groups.

Regardless of whether the right to housing has, or has not been recognized explicitly in the domestic legislation, the most widespread obstacle to the access to housing identified in the reports for the European Observatory on Homelessness and in other research documents, is the insufficient allocation of means, more particularly of financial resources. In three Member States; Denmark, Luxembourg and the Netherlands, national experts estimate that problems associated with the prevention of homelessness and the reintegration of homeless people into housing are not directly related to inadequate allocation of financial resources.

According to Vranken and van Menxel (1994) in Belgium in 1987 some 75,000 households were on the waiting lists for public housing and although more recent data are not available it is reasonable to assume that both waiting lists and waiting time have been increasing. Indeed, public housing was one of the targets of austerity policies and it has become increasingly inaccessible to very low-income groups. The authors refer to the survey conducted by the National Housing Society to show how the Flemish public authorities have halved the investment credits for housing associations between 1980 and 1989.

Specht-Kittler (1994) illustrates the investment slump which is also reflected in the number of newly constructed houses, more particularly in the field of social housing. "Whilst in 1987 there were still approximately 4 million homes, this figure decreased in 1990 to about 2.8 million; experts estimate that by the year 2,000 a further 1.8 million social homes will disappear from the market" (p. 15). This has contributed to a sharp imbalance between the supply and demand for low-cost housing.

Salinas Ramos (1994) underlines that government's allocation of resources is directed towards fiscal measures aimed at subsidizing certain types of loans, but that insignificant resources are oriented towards facilitating access to the rental sector.

De Gouy (1994) attributes the non-implementation of the right to housing in France to administrative problems in identifying target groups, non-implementation of existing legislation, complexity of procedures and lack of coherence in interpretation of legal norms and uncertainty of state funding.

Sapounakis (1994) stresses the shortage of public funding and the drop in public expenditure for housing since 1985. Not only fewer low-interest loans have become available but also the introduction of additional demographic criteria for the access to public housing funds has reduced the number of people eligible for assistance.

Harvey (1995) analyzes why the Housing Act of 1988 did not house Ireland's homeless people and concludes that the legislation was passed "in the year that the local authority building programme was at an historic low point. In 1985, 7,002 local authority houses were built with State finance; in 1988, that figure fell to 768. Even now, it is only claiming back to a target of 3,500 a year" (p. 6). The reasons behind the unfulfilled commitment are found in the non-binding nature of legal provisions and lack of obligation and enforceability which cumulates in the inappropriate allocation of resources.

Tosi and Ranci (1994) stress that marginal and poverty stricken groups encounter obstacles due to the shortcomings in the formal definition of rights, administrative practices and practical difficulties. Groups in severe need are not given adequate consideration for allocation of housing and may even be penalized under conditions of general insufficiency in the supply of low-cost housing.

Marques Balsa and Barreto (1994) show that the official housing policy in Portugal has reflected ideologies of the prevailing political establishments over the course of this century. From the 1980s onward the de-regularization of the housing sector has been associated with a sharp decrease in public and semi-public investment. This has resulted not only in the insufficient supply of low-cost housing but also in the low quality of dwellings and unsatisfactory infrastructure. Rent subsidies intended to accompany liberalization of the market have been granted to a very small group consisting mainly of aged people. In 1988 subsidies were granted to 12,555 persons, and the average age of assisted tenants was 67. One in four were above the age of 75.

Carlisle (1994) identifies the financial regime which housing must operate in as an underlying problem for social housing provision in Britain. The continuing decline in the supply of local authority housing, and the large number of homeless people approaching local authorities has led to heavy demand for the remaining local authority housing. In

1993, 1,204,814 households were on the general waiting list in England. People may be on the waiting list for three years on average.

The provision of means in Denmark, Luxembourg and the Netherlands may be, to a lesser degree, associated with inadequate allocation of financial resources and is more associated with difficulties in implementing a comprehensive approach to a complex "combination of multifactorial social marginalization processes and the individual conditions which drive a person into exclusion and/or homelessness" (Rostgaard and Koch-Nielsen, 1994).

In Luxembourg, however, 10 years of residence in the country as a requirement of access to the minimum non-contributory means, and the high age threshold of 30 years as a condition for eligibility, excludes unemployed immigrants and young adults in precarious living conditions from social solidarity.

De Feijter and Radstaak (1994) affirm that the housing stock is generally estimated to meet the needs in terms of quantity and quality. However, the urban renewal programmes which have contributed to the improvement of the quality of dwellings for the majority of the population, have resulted in the closing down of low-cost boarding houses. These have traditionally provided shelter to the majority of Netherlands's homeless people and their disappearance from the marginal housing market may increase pressure on the public and voluntary services.

1.5. MONITORING OF IMPLEMENTATION

All European Union countries have made a commitment to progressively enhancing the right and access to housing for their citizens. In order to assess the evolution and enforcement of legal instruments and allocation of means "to the maximum of its available resources" (United Nations, 1966), the process needs to be systematically monitored, not only by the governments, but by all parties concerned. The monitoring of implementation imminently goes a step further than the mere assessment of government's will to enhance the right to housing and implies a careful scrutiny of the degree of determination and efficacy of used legal, financial and organizational instruments. The ultimate measure of efficacy of the establishment of the right is the number of people excluded from adequate housing and the harshness of their living conditions.

According to the degree of establishment of the right to housing in their national legislation, countries may be situated along a continuum from inadequacy of legal instruments to address housing exclusion because homeless and no-income people have no access to permanent low-cost housing, to a multitude of empowering legal provisions and a limited number of statutory commitments.

In the four southern European Union countries, Greece, Spain, Italy and Portugal, shortcomings in the establishment of the right to housing are still rooted in the inadequacy of the legal framework providing access to minimum subsistence means and to low-cost housing. It may be said that in some of these countries social housing rights are still supplementary worker's rights, rather than citizen's rights. The social policy measures and access to housing are still tailored for the conditions of growing employment opportunities. They do not address housing exclusion which results from no access to paid labour. The states make no universal commitment to providing non-contributory benefits or to effectively opening access to permanent housing for no-income homeless and badly housed people. In Italy and in Spain, legislation is introduced in some regions, but it stems from the political will of the local authorities, rather than from the comprehensive national anti-poverty and social housing policy. Individuals in difficulty in Greece and Portugal are entirely dependent on family networks and their private coping strategies. The passage from the rent control system to the market conform housing has not been accompanied by individualized financial assistance to low-income groups. Countries have abandoned the concept of affordable housing but have not implemented the non-discretionary individualized solvency-of-the-poor legislation.

In the remaining eight countries, Belgium, Germany, Denmark, France, Ireland, Luxembourg, the Netherlands and the United Kingdom, it may be said that the legal premises for the establishment of the right to housing for non-earning and low-income groups exist. Their scope is to progressively enable homeless and potentially homeless people to claim the right to housing, or to trace a path to desirable schemes by establishing enabling legislative measures. Granting statutory, preferential or simply the right to apply for public housing, cannot solve the complexity of problems associated to homelessness and housing stress of excluded people. But, no durable progress can be made unless the vested right to housing is clearly formulated as a right of all citizens.

However, even a limited insight into legal instruments dealing with access to permanent housing for low-income groups, shows that causes of the failure to implement the right to housing lie outside the legislative framework. This does not mean that the legal instruments are exhaustive, but rather that the existing ones are mostly permissive or enabling rather than mandatory and enforceable. The lack of mechanisms to enforce the legal dispositions makes much of the existing legislation inoperative. In countries which have adopted a legal instrument for the establishment of the right to decent housing, obstacles to its implementation occur when:

-   the law is not applied;
-   inadequate resources are earmarked;
-   certain groups are deliberately excluded;
-   income thresholds for access to publicly funded housing are too high;
-   multiplication of administrative and juridical procedures is not accompanied by the clear identification of duties;
-   social housing favours housing segregation.

The six ambiguities are found throughout the Union. We will illustrate them only by stereotypical examples of how even the most progressive initiatives may be bypassed.

The law which authorizes mayors to requisition abandoned buildings which was passed on 12 January 1993 as part of an urgent programme, has never been applied in Belgium over the past two years. No mayor has resorted to a requisition of an abandoned building in order to refurbish it and allocate it to homeless and badly housed people. One of the reasons may be rooted in the fact that a large part of the abandoned urban housing stock is owned by the communes in the first place, and that resources for refurbishing are not earmarked. The second obstacle is, no doubt, associated with the conflicting nature of the constitutional right of the owners to preserve their property and the constitutional right of the poor to access housing.

The impact of the financial input in social housing may be esteemed as inadequate when we take into account the fact that at least 200,000 new social housing units per year are needed in West Germany, and that the current provision amounts to around 96,000 (Specht-Kittler, 1994).

The Housing Act 1985 in the United Kingdom discriminates against single homeless people who, under the current legislation and instructions for its interpretation, do not qualify for permanent housing.

Income thresholds for social housing in Germany have been increased by approximately 30 per cent as of October 1994. Enlargement of assistance to a broader population base may be a positive development provided that allocated resources are proportionally increased and that legal priority schemes are implemented. When that is not the case, and when more people are forced to compete for the same or even decreased housing stock, the poor and the homeless are bound to be further marginalized by more meritorious groups.

The multiplication of administrative and juridical procedures may result in the paralysis of action. The large number of dispositions under conditions of a low degree of coordination and no clear identification of competence and duties in France, implies that people may be sent back and forth from one instance to another (de Gouy, 1994).

An explicit aim of the general welfare assistance in the Danish housing policy is to ensure a mixed social composition of tenants in the non-profit housing. However, even generous social and housing benefits have not solved problems of concentration of low-income groups and people with social problems in the social housing areas (Rostgaard and Koch-Nielsen, 1994).

The fact that a permissive law is passed in which only principles and enabling instruments are foreseen, but no mandatory obligation to provide is incorporated, may even be derisory. It may propagate a false image of the reality by stressing the formal aspects of protection and masking the lack of implementation. Some experts argue that non-enforceable rights are false rights (Belorgey, 1995). Belorgey affirms that a real right to housing does not exist in France although the law uses the word "right".

> "There is no doubt that the words are the echo of a hope,
> but it is purely a declaration of intent, it is not positive law.
> ... when one gives public opinion and users to believe -

generally the users do not believe in it for very long, but public opinion does, which, psychologically at least, worsens the fate of weak users - when one leads people to believe that there are rights, and there are no rights, I think it is fair to say that one creates a worse situation than when one does not declare any rights" (Belorgey, 1995 p. 172)

One may, indeed, find a multitude of examples of false rights. The legislator has foreseen that the public welfare centres in Belgium may directly provide social housing by engaging in the construction and renovation of dwelling for people they otherwise assist. This, however, should not mislead us to believing that they do so. Indeed, since 1976 when the law was passed, no public welfare centre in Belgium has resorted to the option of renovating or constructing housing (Fierens, 1993). The Irish law enables local authorities to monitor homelessness and housing needs, but does not oblige them to do so consistently or effectively (Harvey, 1994).

The lack of enforceability, the lack of clear identification of responsibilities and duties, the lack of comprehensive identification of target groups, the inconsistent monitoring of implementation, the uncritical evaluation of the efficacy of used legal instruments and policy measure, and the insufficient allocation of resources, form a chain of obstacles in the process of the establishment of the right to housing as an individual entitlement.

1.6. AFFIRMATION AND REAFFIRMATION OF PRINCIPLES

The United Nations Human Rights Fact Sheet includes an information that

"no less than 12 different texts adopted and proclaimed by the United Nations explicitly recognize the right to adequate housing" (Centre for Human Rights, 1993 p.5).

The United Nations agenda illustrates the well established axiom that in order to keep a social issue on the policy program, principles need to be reaffirmed continuously.

Proposals to scrap already acquired rights or to limit access of the undeserved segments of the population, prove that reaffirmation of principles is needed not only to further develop rights, but also to maintain the existing ones. A survey conducted by Shelter in 1993 showed that 80 per cent of local authorities think that the homelessness legislation in the United Kingdom has been successful. The majority affirmed that the system of allocation of housing to homeless people should be improved, not dismantled. Nevertheless, in January 1994 the government issued a proposal for reforming the homelessness legislation in view of making access to social housing more difficult for homeless and potentially homeless people. The opposition from housing organizations and the voluntary sector, and over 10,000 responses to the consultation paper, testify to the determination of social actors and citizens to protect the acquired right to the statutory provision of housing for the homeless people.

Under conditions of conflicting aspirations of different political groups, advantages of social protection based on principles of solidarity need to be continuously reaffirmed. Under conditions of competition for limited social protection resources between individuals, social groups and generations, terms of cooperation and redistribution are continuously under scrutiny and are subject to renegotiation. In the process of reassessment of terms of social protection between state authorities, employers, social partners and concerned social groups, affirmation and reaffirmation of the basic human right to adequate housing is needed to exert moral and political pressures both to maintain the acquired and to implement the promised rights.

Chapter 2

HOMELESSNESS: BREACH OF THE SOCIAL CONTRACT

The social contract which serves as the basic agreement in organized societies, and which regulates relations between members of the society and between citizens and the government, builds on the universal premise that the inherent dignity of a human person will be protected by the principal executive offices of a nation. This protection is to be guaranteed to the maximum of a country's available resources. But, the cumulative effect of the interaction between culture and structure reflected in the type of policy commitment and the nature of acknowledged rights and obligations, imposes also the determination of the degree of urgency of their implementation.

The European Union countries have defined common objectives and have already, in the preamble to the Treaty of the European Union (1992), expressed their determination to promote economic and social progress of their people. Article 2 of the Treaty defines the key common aim to be pursued: high level of employment and high standard of social security. The same Article includes a policy commitment to the promotion of the standard of living and quality of life of citizens, as well as to the economic and social solidarity between Member States. The Treaty clearly reflects the intention of Member States to pursue the development of social security, but it fails to include a commitment to the minimum standards of social protection. The task of developing common social security and setting minimum standards was envisioned as part of a complementary agreement. Indeed, the policy commitment to adequate social protection and to the struggle against social exclusion is made in the Agreement on Social Policy (Article 1) which as a Protocol is an Appendix to the Treaty. In order to implement the common aims, 11 Member States (United Kingdom has not adopted the Agreement) agreed to support and to complement actions of the Member States in integrating people excluded from the labour market. Although no specific mention is made to housing exclusion, it is evident that social security inherently encompasses a housing dimension. The key issue here is not whether all the components of social protection and all the conditions of social exclusion are explicitly enumerated in the Agreement, but whether degrees of urgency of social action to combat exclusion are determined.

A high level of employment and high level of social security are defined in the Maastricht Treaty as general aims for the realization of which no specific time-limit can be set. While the pursuit of high standards may be set as a goal to be achieved in an unspecified future, protection of minimum standards requires a commitment not only to the goal, but also to the urgency of its implementation. Indeed, general societal goals may be measured against time in its historical perspective, but the impact of protection policies on individuals needs to be seen in their day-to-day efficacy. Limits of one human life-span impose a measure of urgency in the provision of the most basic human needs. Combatting social exclusion, even when formulated only as a statement of intent, is a binding obligation to alleviate here-and-now its extreme consequences. Housing the homeless people is a task to be measured by days, months and years of an individual's life.

Even at times of a slow-down in economic growth, the incidence of homelessness in the European Union countries which are among the richest in the world, may be considered as a breach of the social contract between citizens and authorities. The existence of structurally induced housing exclusion is evidence of the government's failure to prioritize and to provide for the most vulnerable. Homeless people excluded from housing and from community care are the ultimate victims of the breach of the social contract.

Homelessness in the European Union countries is the most visible evidence of the failure of policies to prevent extreme poverty and social exclusion, as well as of the inefficacy of palliative measures to reintegrate the excluded into housing, into labour, into a family and social network. Both aggregate analysis and individual histories testify that once social exclusion reaches the stage of homelessness, the obstacles to reintegration increase and acquire additional structural, juridical, civil, social and psychological dimensions. Indeed, data show that as the duration of the condition of homelessness increases, the cumulative effect of exclusion aggravates reintegration of homeless people (Council of Europe, 1993; Daly, 1994; McCarthy, 1988; Filosa, 1993).

Homeless people are those unable to access and maintain a personal dwelling from their own resources, but they are by no means the only people excluded from adequate housing. Badly housed people, who cannot access decent housing due to their income insufficiency, form the outer core of housing exclusion. The degree of harshness of living conditions of people who cannot compete in the formal housing market is the ultimate measure of the degree of urgency of social protection.

2.1. PEOPLE WHO CANNOT COMPETE ON THE FORMAL HOUSING MARKET

The right to housing approach pursued in Chapter 1 necessitates a comprehensive analysis of housing exclusion. The right, as defined in major international standard-setting documents and domestic legislation, addresses the right to adequate housing and not just the right to shelter. Consequently, not only the people sleeping rough or in shelters for homeless people or squatting, but, also badly housed people constitute the population whose rights are breached because they cannot access adequate housing with their own resources. However, the extent and the type of external constraints and obstacles encountered, as well as the type of social assistance necessary to remove impediments, will vary according to the degree of housing exclusion. They will also determine whether housing exclusion is of a transitory or permanent nature. Thus, identifying the population sub-groups who cannot compete on the formal housing market according to a variety of conditions observed at one point in time and according to the type of obstacles they encounter, will be the first step in the analysis of the process of housing exclusion.

The concept of housing exclusion is intrinsically linked to the concept of adequate housing. It is in relation to housing norms and housing standards which have become accessible to the majority of the population that we can define the condition of those who are excluded. Thus, in one of the more prosperous sub-regions of Europe, a home no longer implies "four walls and a roof" but criteria of affordability, quality and security of tenure form a borderline separating those with a home from people excluded from adequate housing. In the economic and legal reality of the European Union at the turn of the 21st century, people excluded from adequate housing are those who are excluded from legal, affordable, sanitary dwellings, with a secure tenure and minimum space to meet the needs of the household.

Within the sub-population which is excluded from adequate housing because it is unable to compete on the formal housing market, different degrees of harshness of living conditions separate people who have lost access to a dwelling from other population sub-groups who live under high housing stress due to bad housing conditions. However, the homeless and those under severe housing stress share the common reality of people who, due to their income insufficiency and lack of affordable good quality housing, are experiencing social marginalization and may be exposed to progressive exclusion from the most important domains of human activity. Both homelessness and bad housing are factors of life and health threatening environmental hazards (Satterthwaite, 1995). Exposure to environmental hazards due to the lack of a home or over-crowding, disrepair, no access to sanitary facilities, environmental degradation, is associated to ill health, disability, psychological stress, developmental constrains, lower life expectancy, housing and social segregation, and may be associated to obstacles in accessing the social deliveries of services ranging from education and health care to culture and leisure.

2.1.1. Homelessness and bad housing: conditions, concepts and definitions

Attempts to provide a universal definition of the condition of homelessness generally end in a sophisticism characterizing homelessness as a manifestation of a multitude of conditions which may be an outcome of a variety of events. Indeed, a comprehensive analysis of the phenomenon of homelessness necessitates insight into living conditions which near anything from sleeping rough to overcrowding, and determinants which may range from natural or man made disaster to an individual's choice to be freed from his home. Among policy makers, the criteria to identify the condition and alleviate its consequences are largely founded on the evaluation of causes of homelessness and the perception of potential threats to social cohesion. Events which are beyond control of individuals, such as natural disaster, will result in a relatively high degree of consensus about the unacceptability of the condition and the need to assist victims. Events which are equally beyond the individual's control such as structurally induced long-term unemployment, housing shortage or deinstitutionalization of mental health care, still raise disputes about the extent of social solidarity that should be extended to victims.

In many European Union countries the concept of homelessness has only recently entered into the political and legislative vocabulary. Governments still seem to find it difficult to acknowledge the existence of extreme poverty within prosperous economies, and are inclined to underestimate its magnitude. They are willing to define the social condition of homelessness only in administrative terms as predetermined (non) eligibility for assistance, rather than to identify diversified population sub-groups in need of permanent housing. The ideology of the deserving versus the undeserving poor largely underlines pragmatic definitions of homelessness. In Ireland and the United Kingdom, on the one hand, homeless people are officially recognized only on the basis of criteria set out by the authorities who identify groups in housing need or potentially eligible for housing assistance. Homeless applicants for housing in the United Kingdom need to prove to the local authorities that they are unintentionally homeless, through no fault of their own. On the other hand, in Italy, Spain, Greece, Portugal, no specific reference to the social condition of homelessness is made in provisions defining access to housing. In all cases the homeless are undercounted.

By way of example, the authorities in the United Kingdom officially accepted 159,974 households as homeless or potentially homeless in 1993 (Department of Environment, Welsh office and Scottish Office, 1993). If we use the average household size as a basis on which to estimate the number of homeless people, the figure stands at close to 384,000 people. While this figure corresponds to the number of people who were officially recognized as being excluded from adequate housing and eligible for assistance it does not include all homeless people. It does not include people who were assessed to be homeless through their own fault, and it does not include single homeless people who could not afford a dwelling and resorted to different accommodation arrangements from shelters and hostels, to doubling up with friends and relatives. The number of single homeless people in London alone is estimated at 140,000 (Spaull, 1992). CRISIS (1995) reports that every single night there are over 17,000 people in temporary accommodation in London hostels and night shelters. Estimates of the number of single homeless people for the country as a whole are not available. In England and Wales the actual number of households that applied for housing as homeless was 352,394 and the number of people living in these households can be estimated at 845,000. The local authorities accepted as homeless in England and Wales only four out of 10 applicants, i.e. 145,411 households. Some 3.5 million properties are described as being in need of major repairs (Department of Environment, 1993). Information about the condition of the housing stock translated into living conditions of people means that as many as 8.4 million people may be badly housed.

On the basis of an Italian survey on poverty, the estimated number of people with no fixed abode stands at between 50,000 and 61,000. In order to assess the magnitude of homelessness Tosi affirms that at least 70,000 homeless immigrants should be added. The minimum number of homeless people is estimated by the author - on the basis of data regarding only four categories of extremely poor persons: those with no fixed abode, immigrants, gypsies, and mental patients - as between 150,000 and 220,000. According to Tosi (1993) some 500,000 people living in extreme poverty are under severe housing stress. If we look at the number of people who cannot afford to live in dwellings with minimum sanitary facilities then we arrive at an estimate that 1.1 million Italians in the late 1980s did not have a toilet in their dwelling and 9 million people did not have an inside bath or a shower (Tables 3 and 4).

In order to agree on the number of people excluded from adequate housing we need to agree on the socially acceptable standards of adequacy of dwellings. In order to agree on the number of homeless people we need to reach a consensus that the "invisible" and the "undeserving" homeless, those who do not figure on the authority's lists of people eligible for public assistance, are also people in need of adequate housing.

In the minds of many people, homelessness is identified with the condition of tramps and vagrants. Research results are often received with scepticism. "Where are those hundreds of thousands of homeless people? If they are not in the streets, they are not homeless", is a typical reaction. At best, homelessness will be identified with the condition of people having no fixed abode. But, women with dependent children and young adults, the two fastest growing homeless sub-groups, victims of poverty, domestic violence, sexual abuse, family conflicts and other traumatic events, usually have a formal abode, but do not have a home. Indeed, the homeless population extends far beyond the most visible condition of those sleeping rough and those classified administratively as people lacking abode. They are in fact the smallest, even though the most visible, part of the homeless population.

The research into homeless has advanced sufficiently so that greater order in the definition of concepts and conditions can be made. The cumulative effect of research of housing exclusion is a solid basis for the identification of the subject and for the development of the appropriate research methodology.

People sleeping rough account for only a small fraction of homeless people. They are also only a fraction of people with no fixed abode. The Italian Poverty Survey showed that three out of 10 people without a fixed abode usually slept in dormitories, two in improper housing, three anywhere and only four out of 100 people without a fixed abode were usually sleeping rough in public places (Tosi and Ranci, 1994). People in temporary shelters provided by the public and voluntary services and those in rented rooms on short term basis who have no security of shelter and no prospects to access a personal dwelling, are the most numerous part of the nucleus of homelessness. People assisted by the public and voluntary sector because they have no home, and on their own could not afford any accommodation, are those who have exhausted their private coping strategies and are dependent on social solidarity. Those paying for their precarious accommodation in rented rooms often in sub-standard housing or bed and breakfast are those who are able to pay for their own temporary shelter but have no access to a home.

When observing the homeless population at one point in time we may identify a series of accommodation situations. But, it is necessary to acknowledge that over time people who cannot access a personal dwelling move between different forms of housing exclusion. Furthermore, the condition of homelessness varies greatly in duration. Homelessness may be transitory or it may become a permanent condition. Indeed, when data on housing histories of people who have experienced homelessness are available, they show that homeless people have been, or are, pendulating between public and voluntarily run shelters, boarding houses, furnished rooms at the margin of regular rental accommodation, shacks, squats, and casual doubling up with friends and relatives.

Homeless people are compelled to be the most spatially mobile of the excluded. Being allowed to stay in sheltered accommodation only for a limited duration and being able to afford and find casual accommodation on short term basis they will pendulate between different forms of housing exclusion. Typically, individuals will move frequently from one accommodation arrangement to another. Thus, there may be no clear cut line separating those people who have no accommodation, who are in temporary accommodation in dormitories, boarding houses or hotels provided as urgent shelter by the public or voluntary organizations, from those in precarious dwellings at the margin of the regular rental market. People without a dwelling may move between situations which near anything from sleeping rough, squatting, staying in urgent accommodation provided by public and voluntary organizations which may be shelters for homeless people or hostels, guest houses, asylums and hospital annexes.

Identification of the common denominators of a multitude of conditions of homelessness is the theoretical basis for the definition of the condition of homelessness and identification of homeless people as used in our analysis. Homelessness is defined as the lack of access to adequate personal accommodation. Homeless people are those who are unable to access and maintain an adequate personal dwelling from their own resources, and people unable to maintain personal accommodation unless secured community care.

We will delimit our analysis to two manifest forms of the phenomenon of homelessness, namely homelessness as the outcome of the social process of impoverishment which results in exclusion of the poor from adequate housing, and homelessness as the outcome of exclusion from community care which results in the inability of people in need of care to maintain a personal dwelling. Poverty, adequate housing and adequate care, are perceived in their historical dimension. Poverty is understood as a lack of money, material possessions and opportunity. Normative standards about adequate housing and adequate care are perceived in the light of the overall level of development, predominant societal values, group access to resources, and individuals' access to resources, as well as individuals' needs, values and choices.

Exclusion from personal accommodation defines the condition of homelessness. Exclusion from adequate housing in terms of quality and security defines the condition of badly housed people, those living in insanitary, sub-standard, overcrowded, insecure dwellings. It may not always be possible to draw a clear line between the living conditions of homeless people who turn to the public and voluntary shelters, from those living in "unconventional dwellings" or "other types of dwellings", euphemisms used to name shacks, cellars, staircases, containers, tents and caravans. This will particularly be the case in countries and regions where shelters for people who have no access to adequate housing are scarce and where homeless people have to improvise their "unconventional dwellings".

On the basis of data available for the European Union countries concerning the quality of dwellings, it is not possible to delimit, with precision, thresholds of housing segmentation which delimit housing stress. For the initial identification of badly housed people we will use several indicators to identify housing inadequacy. Namely, access to sanitary infrastructure within a dwelling, the ratio between the number of persons and the number of rooms per dwelling, and the state of disrepair of dwellings. For badly housed people housing stress is generally marked by the overlapping of several precarious conditions. Sub-standard accommodation and overcrowding tend to coincide, sub-standard dwellings will frequently be without sanitary facilities, insecurity of tenure may affect any of those conditions. This makes research into living conditions, socio-demographic characteristics and proximate determinants of housing exclusion particularly difficult. However, in order to identify the outer core of housing exclusion we will focus on the condition which delimits severe housing stress. This condition will be identified either in terms of overcrowding or sub-standard housing depending on available data.

2.1.2. Data sources on homelessness and bad housing

For the time being, in the Member States of the European Union, data on homelessness come mainly from service providers and from isolated researchers (Table 1). Data from service providers enable us to partially quantify the magnitude and identify characteristics of homeless people who have been assisted, but not of those who were left out of the system of public and voluntary solidarity. Only targeted social research of housing exclusion, which would include primary data collecting and access to relevant housing, social and health statistics, could document homelessness in a comprehensive way.

Up to now, no European Union country has undertaken a complete count of homeless people and of those under severe housing stress. Population and household censuses, generally undertaken at 10 or five year intervals, are not a sufficient instrument for monitoring housing exclusion. A population census registers people according to the place they happen to be on the day of the census. Therefore, a census can catch some but not all conditions of exclusion from adequate housing. Indeed, due to the methodological limitations inherent to population and household censuses, a significant part of the homeless population is left out of the count. Furthermore, time-spans between censuses, of 5 to 10 years, are much too long. Homelessness, as a burning social issue, needs to be monitored and socially addressed on continuous basis.

Most statistical offices gather information about housing conditions of households. Thus, housing statistics could document exclusion from adequate housing of badly housed people. However, they are not always made available, and, furthermore, have not been standardized at the European Union level. The European Household Panel Study initiated under EUROSTAT's coordination may be expected to provide some data to document bad housing conditions and housing-related expenditures which may fragilize socially vulnerable households. However, a general panel can include a very small number of socially marginal groups and risks to encounter a high no-response rate, more particularly by those threatened by homelessness.

Data collected by the state and by housing authorities about applicants and recipients of housing assistance, even when available, are incomplete. Governments have not been willing to dispatch national statistics about the number and characteristics of people who were homeless but have been rehoused, those on waiting lists and those who have been refused housing assistance. They have been even less willing to gather information about homeless people who do not qualify and thus do not even apply for state assistance.

Table 1: An overview of quantitative sources on homelessness available in 1994

COUNTRY	YEAR[1]	SERVICE PRO-VIDERS	SECONDARY SOURCES	OFFICIAL COUNTS	
				ALL HOME LESS	SOME CATEGO-RIES
BELGIUM	1993	yes	yes	n.a.[2]	n.a.
DENMARK	1992	yes	yes	n.a.	n.a.
GERMANY	1994	yes	yes	n.a.	n.a.
SPAIN	1991	n.a.	yes	n.a.	n.a.
FRANCE	1993	yes	yes	n.a.[3]	n.a.
GREECE	1993	n.a.	yes	n.a.	n.a.
IRELAND	1993	yes	yes	n.a.	yes
ITALY	1994	n.a.	yes	n.a.	n.a.
LUXEMBOURG	1994	yes	yes	n.a.	n.a.
NETHERLANDS	1994	yes	yes	n.a.	n.a.[4]
PORTUGAL	1993	n.a.	yes	n.a.	n.a.
UK	1993	yes	yes	n.a.	yes

Note-worthy are projects to standardize information from shelters in the Netherlands (KLIMOP, 1994) and the multidisciplinary approach in setting up a data collection system to document homelessness and housing exclusion in France (CNIS, 1994). The statistical office of the European Union EUROSTAT is expected to monitor these national

---

1   Latest available data.

2   n.a. = non available

3   The project of the Conseil National de l'Information Statistique (CNIS) has been launched for the 1994-1998 period with the aim of collecting data on homelessness in France.

4   The computerised data collection system KLIMOP was launched in 1994 with the aim of pooling and standardizing data from service providers.

initiatives and to evaluate the feasibility of similar projects in other European Union countries.

If significant progress is to be made in order to monitor, analyze and socially address the issue of homelessness in a comprehensive way, a serious effort needs to be made by the authorities and by the scientific community to pool data from different statistical sources and to implement targeted primary research of homelessness.

However, the scarcity of reliable analytical data can be partially compensated by a critical evaluation of available data sources and a prudent analysis. Thus, whilst one needs to be cautious when drawing conclusions and more particularly cross country comparisons, on the basis of incomplete data or diversified sources, the analytical information and the overall body of knowledge form a valuable base for the formulation of tentative hypotheses' about the magnitude of housing exclusion, general tendencies observed over time, and background and proximate determinants of homelessness.

Data from population and household censuses provide limited data on housing conditions. Identification of badly housed people exposed to a high degree of housing stress in insanitary, sub-standard, overcrowded dwellings, without juridical and financial security of tenure, who account for the overwhelming majority of people excluded from adequate housing, will be based on these censuses. Due to the fact that several precarious conditions may overlap, it is extremely difficult to assess the magnitude of the population under high housing stress. However, data from population and household censuses and household surveys provide sufficient basis for tentative estimates of the extent of bad housing and of the magnitude of the population affected by severe housing stress.

Preliminary research enables us to formulate a general hypothesis about the cumulative effect of multiple forms of social exclusion on housing conditions of people and on their housing strategies. This approach imminently goes beyond focusing on a particular condition which may be observed at one point in time, and is based on the analysis of the social process leading to the condition of housing exclusion. An analysis of housing exclusion which would focus only on the homeless people who sleep outside dwelling units or in temporary shelter, would give a much too narrow perception of the phenomenon of exclusion from adequate housing today. It may give only a snapshot of the population which has no access to minimum standards of decent living and housing. A narrow focus on people sleeping rough and in shelters for homeless people reduces the problem of housing provision to temporary accommodation and services for the marginalized sector of homeless people. By contrast, an analysis of multiple forms of housing exclusion provides both a solid base for the development of comprehensive policy strategies to reintegrate homeless people into adequate housing, and also to prevent homelessness and to progressively integrate badly housed people into adequate housing.

There is insufficient research evidence to establish a causal link between exclusion from adequate housing and homelessness. It cannot be taken for granted that badly housed people are more at risk of becoming homeless than other vulnerable groups. What, however, is the common denominator of the condition of homelessness and other forms of housing exclusion is the income insufficiency as an obstacle to access to, and to maintenance of, adequate housing. Both homelessness and bad housing expose people to environmental hazards. Depending on the degree of disrepair or overcrowding, bad housing results in housing stress and may be associated with several environmental hazards. Health risks of environmental hazards are quite well known from research undertaken by doctors and psychologists but are less well documented in other disciplines. Aggregated data on morbidity and mortality according to the housing condition and housing history would, no doubt, be better indicators of the quality of housing, than size, type of construction, or equipment of the dwellings. There are strong arguments in favour of the use of life expectancy, rather than classical economic indicators, to document the condition of poverty (Sen, 1995). There is a clear need for the research of homelessness and bad housing to cut across disciplines and to resort to demographic, as well as economic and housing indicators. However, data needed for more sophisticated statistical analysis are not available. We have to rely largely on contextual data.

The extent of risks associated to bad housing become widely recognized usually only at times of flood, earthquake or fire. Bad housing may be a potential risk situation for the occupants, but it may also result in environmental degradation. The rainstorms in Greece in 1994 not only left families homeless but the resulting floods in Athens were partly attributed to the lack of efficient urban planning and the extent of substandard housing. Inefficient planning and inability to control illegal building is estimated to have partly caused and increased the toll of the natural disaster (Sapounakis, 1994).

2.2. THE CONDITION OF HOMELESSNESS

Those who turn to public or voluntary organizations for street work services, emergency accommodation or priority rehousing because they are unable to help themselves, constitute the most disadvantaged social group in economically advanced countries. Whichever criterion of poverty level and social exclusion one may operate with, whether EUROSTAT (1990), O'Higgins and Jenkins (1990), Deleeck et al. (1990), or however we may measure the income inadequacy, as primary poverty line (Rowntree, 1901) or socio-vital minimum (Vranken, 1972), there is no doubt that the population which has no access whatsoever to legal, affordable and secure personal dwellings is the most excluded and disentitled population subgroup in modern societies.

Having no dwelling is the state of extreme lack of means and opportunity. It is a condition which in its turn brings even further exclusion to those homeless people who do not have a fixed abode and who may be denied access to welfare assistance and minimum income and encounter obstacles in access to primary health care, personal documents and political rights (Sachar, 1992; Drake, 1994; Daly, 1994). If we transpose Turner's (1976) observation about housing in general to the condition of those sleeping rough or in establishments which shelter the homeless, one could conclude that the important thing to be said about homelessness is not what it is, but what it does to peoples' lives.

For individuals homelessness may be a situation experienced during a particular time in the life course. Teenagers in search of identity may leave a parental home to join the peer group and spend some time in particular districts of large cities. People discharged from psychiatric institutions, faced with solitude and need of care, may turn to shelters for homeless people or may squat with others. Breakdown of a relationship, more particularly when associated to domestic violence, may result in loss of a dwelling. Homelessness may indeed be a condition which people experience for relatively short periods of time, but it may be a durable exclusion which marks the final stage of social marginalization.

No data are available about the duration of the state of having no dwelling which would be representative on the national or transnational levels. In Denmark, a country which may be considered as the forerunner in social and housing provisions and where homelessness is least associated to a rift between minimum income and housing costs, it is estimated that people may remain homeless for 2-4 years (Brandt, 1992). Data from a shelter on the duration of stay of homeless people show that only one in 10 residents stayed less than a week, four out of 10 stayed up to three months, three out of 10 up to one year, and two out of 10 stayed in shelters more than one year (Danish National Institute of Social Research, 1994). In the Flemish community in Belgium four out of 10 sheltered homeless people stay in a shelter up to 10 days. The majority of people, six out of 10 stay less than one month (Thuislozenzorg, 1993). A similar pattern, although less well empirically documented, is observed for the French speaking part of Belgium. Thus, it may be tentatively concluded that for the majority of people who experience homelessness it is a transitory state, and that homelessness is a permanent state only for a minority.

The fact that, for the majority of people who experience homelessness it may be a transitory state, does not make it less important. The devastating impact of homelessness needs to be perceived not only in terms of the duration of the condition but also of the time in the individual's life cycle when it occurs. Homelessness is experienced increasingly at the delicate moment of the passage into adulthood. It is at the precise time when young adults need to establish personal relations, access economic activity and enter early stages of the family building processes, that homelessness marks their life prospects. Homelessness experienced by young families, which is also on the rise, marks the life of several generations (ATD Quart Monde, 1995).

There has been no comprehensive research in the Member States about trajectories into and out of homelessness. On the basis of available data from service providers and small-scale research or one-day censuses, we can indirectly trace typical stages leading to homelessness: from underprivileged origin, to exclusion from education, exclusion from work, exclusion from lasting relationships, exclusion from housing and exclusion from opportunities. The sequence of events does not necessarily indicate a direct causal link, but it does point to the relevance of comprehensive research into proximate determinants of homelessness, and to the need for multi-faceted policy response.

For the overwhelming majority, the way into homelessness is associated with income insufficiency and lack of access to affordable housing, and, the condition is generally precipitated by one or more traumatic events in the individual's life. The condition of homelessness, in turn, makes traumatic events a constant in a person's life. The way individuals cope with external constraints and traumatic events, before and after becoming homeless, depends not only on the objective circumstances but also on their personality characteristics. Thus, the way out of homelessness may require social healing which cannot be limited to housing provision.

From indirect sources, namely general research of poverty (Dehaes, 1994), it may be concluded that it is the duration of the process of income insufficiency which distinguishes those who cannot afford a decent dwelling from other sub-groups living below the poverty line. Typically, some 12 per cent of the poor have been poor for more than 10 years (Bane and Ellwood, 1986; Dehaes, 1994). This group may be said to constitute the socially vulnerable pool of people acutely exposed to the risk of not being able to afford a decent dwelling. However, in the chain of determinants of homelessness, the impact of chronic poverty is not easy to measure. Not only the long-lasting income insufficiency but also intergenerational transfer of low skills together with other consequences of poverty, stem out as proximate determinants of homelessness. Personality characteristics may precipitate the passage from marginalization to housing exclusion.

The chronically poor exceed by far in number the homeless population and the two groups do not necessarily coincide. Specific events in a person's life and personality characteristics leading to deviant behaviour, may also precipitate the fall into homelessness of those who were not necessarily exposed to chronic poverty in the family of origin. Even though a causal link between chronic poverty and homelessness is difficult to measure, it may be said that the chain of determinants of extreme exclusion is generally formed by the passage from durable income insufficiency to social marginalization, lack of community care and homelessness. It is precisely the cumulative effect of poverty preceding the condition of homelessness, and, exposure to the deprivation experienced by the homeless, which makes the social reintegration of the homeless people particularly difficult.

Once a personal dwelling is lost, individuals share the objective reality of their condition of homelessness and they share a series of markers of group identity. Some can only be identified but not quantified at aggregate level, others can be documented along broad lines. What we can document by data from service providers for homeless in the 12 European Union countries are some characteristics of people who turn to public or voluntary services for shelter. The available data do not enable us to generalize about the totality of the homeless population for several reasons: because people can use shelters only if a place is available, they will use them as the last resort, often when they are under extreme physical and psychological stress, and the organizational set up of shelters will shape the profile of users. Many people who cannot afford a personal dwelling rely on their private coping strategies and may turn to friends and relatives or sleep rough and squat, and never use a shelter for homeless people. This will be a particularly prevalent strategy in southern European countries where there are very few shelters for homeless people. Athens, a town with an estimated population of 3,6 million in 1995, has 45 beds in shelters for homeless people.

People who are accepted in shelters are those who comply with specific criteria which public and charitable service providers establish. Most shelters will not accommodate paperless immigrants, although some may tacitly break the rules by not asking for the origin or documents of a homeless person. Some shelters will not accept adolescents, others may refuse shelter to drug-addicts. Some institutions operate as shelters and health care centres and will provide medical assistance, others will not take a homeless person with health problems. A homeless woman with a dependent child may be sheltered separately from her teenage son. It is clear that not every shelter for homeless people can assist all the victims and that service providers have to make choices as to whom they may best help. The socio-demographic features of homeless people will reflect more the *credo* and organizational set up of shelters than an objective profile of homeless people.

Available data about people who have turned to public or voluntary services for temporary shelter do not give a straight forward answer to the question of how many people are homeless in the European Union today. Neither can data from shelters and other service providers be used to estimate the number of people who may have experienced homelessness at some point in their life. Data from service providers and secondary research sources cannot be used for sophisticated methods of statistical analysis. Service providers are neither equipped nor qualified to collect statistical information and to set up systems of data processing. This is not their task.

Only pooling of information and standardization of data from all public and voluntary services could provide a representative base for a statistically correct analysis of socio-demographic characteristics of the sheltered homeless population and a systematic count of homeless people who depend on them. This requires a political will of state authorities, allocation of financial resources, and assignment of the data processing task to the competent statistical offices. For the time being, efforts to document homelessness come mainly from isolated researchers and service providers, and only exceptionally from public authorities. Furthermore, the few official counts have included only some categories of homeless people.

2.2.1. Estimates of the extent of homelessness

Estimates of the extent of homelessness in each of the 12 European Union countries made in the early 1990s provide eight qualitatively different types of information. Each of these sources documents some accommodation situations and points to the different conditions and perspectives for homeless people. The available sources are:

- projections based on a statistical model (Germany, Netherlands);
- population census (France);
- official assessment of homelessness by local authorities (Ireland);
- households accepted for housing by local authorities under legislation on homelessness (United Kingdom);
- poverty survey and population census (Italy);
- turnover of users of shelters for homeless people in one year (Belgium, Spain);
- count of users of services on one particular day in a year (Denmark, Luxembourg);
- researchers field experience (Greece, Portugal).

Belgium: The number of times people were registered upon entry in temporary shelters for homeless people stood at 23,937 in 1993. In the Dutch speaking community 12,465 (Thuislozenzorg, 1993) and in the French speaking community 11,472 times homeless people (Association des Maisons d'Accueil, 1993) turned to shelters for accommodation. The number of people who passed through shelters in 1993 is lower than in the previous year. This, however, does not automatically mean that the number of homeless people has decreased. A lower number of users can reflect longer stays in shelters by those homeless people who could access them.

Since homeless people may move from one temporary shelter to another during the course of one year, the figure reflects the turnover of people in these institutions and cannot be interpreted as the total number of homeless people. The number of people who passed through shelters depends on the number of available beds and on the duration of stay of homeless people.

The average duration of stay in shelters was 75 days for men, 43 for women and 39 days for children. If the average duration of stay is estimated at two months (Renard, 1994), the figure for Belgium implies that approximately 4,000 people per day are sheltered in centres for homeless people.

Germany: The estimate by Ruhstrat and Geertsema (1994) based on stock data of houselessness known to the communes in West Germany and by BAG Wohnungslosenhilfe e.V.(1992), is used as a model by Specht-Kittler (1994) to estimate the number of people who have been houseless over a one year period in the Federal Republic. The base year for the projection is 1992 and the figure for 1994 is estimated at 876,450 houseless people. The figure includes 312,000 so-called Aussiedlers from eastern Europe who have been living for 3-5 years in substitute shelters provided by the public bodies. The estimate on a flow basis over a one year period for the old Lander is 842,400, and 34,050 for the new Lander. The estimate of the stock by Specht-Kittler (1994) suggests that the houseless stock in the Old Lander was 468,000 and in the New Lander 22,700.

Denmark: A one day census undertaken in October 1993, where both private and public service providers were asked to provide a statement about the number of users of their services, covered 143 help programmes and encompassed 4,341 users. This figure gives an indication of the extent of social exclusion in the municipality of Copenhagen (Rostgaard and Koch-Nielsen, 1994).

The latest available data on the extent of homelessness come from a one day census undertaken on 15 January 1992 when 2,947 homeless people were in temporary public accommodation and were assisted by 76 reception centres (Denmark Statistik, 1993). On the basis of data from shelters and personal research, Brandt (1994) estimates that some 7,200 people are homeless in Denmark and that on the average people are homeless for 2 to 4 years.

Spain: A survey among people who had been admitted into shelters between 1988 and 1990 showed that the annual average number of homeless people in urgent accommodation was 43,000. In addition, estimates made by researchers bring the number of vagrants to between 40,000 and 45,000 people (Salinas Ramos, 1993). In 1994 Caritas alone has provided diversified types of assistance to 160,000 needy people.

France: In the census of 1990 the number of people registered as having no fixed abode stood at 98,000 and the number of people in shelters for urgent accommodation at 59,000 (Préel, 1992). In addition 45,000 people were registered as living in cellars, shacks, or abandoned buildings. This implies that some 202,000 people were homeless on the day of the census.

For the estimation of the total number of homeless people for FEANTSA's 1993 report on homelessness, data provided in Préels' report on the number of people excluded from housing, and the number of people in furnished rooms and boarding houses privately rented on short-term basis were used. The 202,000 people excluded from housing and the 470,000 in furnished rooms and boarding houses, brought the figure of those estimated to be homeless to 672,000 people.

On the basis of suggestions received from the voluntary sector Chassériaud (1993) estimates that the number of homeless people may stand at 250,000.

Greece: The accommodation centres in Athens organized by the state provide 45 beds all together. The maximum duration of stay in these shelters is three months. If the average duration of two months is used as the base for the estimate of the number of people who have passed through shelters, the figure stands at 270. Sapounakis (1994) estimates that 2,500 people are accommodated in hostels and guest houses for needy people which are sponsored by different organizations. In addition some 1,000 people without a personal dwelling may be staying in boarding houses where they pay for their room. An estimated number of 2,000 people are squatting.

Ireland: According to the official assessment of homelessness conducted by the local authorities in March 1991, there were a total of 2,751 homeless persons over the age of 18. The assessment carried out two years later, in March 1993, put the figure at 2,667 persons, i.e. a decrease of 3 percent over a two year period. Due to the methodological shortcomings, these figures are severely criticized by researchers, and due to little consultation with the voluntary organizations providing services for the homeless the figures are disputed by the voluntary sector. The voluntary sector estimated that some 5,000 people are homeless (O'Sullivan, 1994).

The assessment of local authority housing needs in 1993 identified 2,172 individuals as homeless people eligible for public housing assistance. This is an increase of over 30 per cent in comparison to 1989 when 1,491 homeless people were identified as those in housing need. The difference in the number of people assessed to be homeless and the number of homeless people assessed to be in housing need in 1993, shows that some 21 per cent of people over the age of 18 estimated to be homeless by the local authorities have not been included in the estimation of those in need of permanent accommodation.

Italy: According to data from the Survey of Extreme Poverty (National Commission on Poverty, 1992), the estimated number of people with no fixed abode in 1991 was between 50,486 and 61,753. According to Tosi and Ranci (1994) no abode is identified with homelessness but in reality it refers only to marginalized homeless often identified with vagrants. Homelessness is estimated by the authors to affect at least 150,000-220,000 people. This figure includes immigrants, gypsies and mental patients.

Luxembourg: The answer to a parliamentarian question about the number of homeless people was that there is no exact figure detailing the extent of homelessness or the evolution of the phenomenon (Ministère d'Etat,

1993). The number of people accommodated in the main shelters was reported to be 608 in 1993. A survey conducted by the Centre for the Study of Population, Poverty and Socio-Economic Policies identified 28 shelters and service providers for homeless people in 1994. Only 22 participated in the survey and in the month of May the total number of surveyed homeless people stood at 194.

Netherlands: In 1989 the Dutch Council of Local Authorities estimated the number of homeless people to be between 17,500 to 24,200. The projection model which builds on the research project (Heydendael et al., 1990) gives the number of homeless people in 1989 at between 26,000 and 34,000. The statistical model anticipated that the number of homeless people will reach 53,000 by the year 2000. Interpolation of data up to the end of 1994 by de Feijter and Radstaak (1994) brings the number of homeless people to between 38,500 and 46,500.

In estimating the extent of homelessness, the projection model also included people in temporary accommodation in the commercial circle. People in furnished rooms and boarding houses paying for their accommodation, as well as people dependent on public and voluntary services, were included in the projection. It was estimated that approximately 30 per cent of the homeless population depends on the public and voluntary sector. This implies that in 1994 between 10,000 and 12,000 homeless people may have been dependent on sheltered accommodation.

Portugal: The population census of 1991 registered 600 people as living in cellars, staircases, elevator cages and similar locations. This may be considered as the most official estimation of the number of homeless people *sensu stricto* (Marques Balsa and Barreto, 1994). The estimate based on information from service providers brings the number of people who have been sheltered as homeless in the course of 1993 to 2,870 (Nascimento, 1993).

United Kingdom: The Department of Environment, Welsh Office and Scottish Office registered 159,974 households which were accepted by local authorities as homeless in 1993. If the average household size is used as the basis for the estimation, the figure brings the number of homeless people accepted for housing by the local authorities to 384,000 people. This figure includes neither households judged to be intentionally homeless nor single homeless people who were found not to be eligible for housing. The number of households accepted as homeless under the legislation fell by 7.5 per cent between 1992 and 1993. The decrease in England was 6 percent, in Scotland 25 percent, whilst in Wales the number increased by 8.5 percent. It is, however, premature to conclude on determinants of changes in the number of households accepted for housing. It may, indeed, imply that less households were exposed to homelessness and extreme housing stress in 1993, but it may also imply that local authorities applied more severe standards in defining priority need groups eligible for the allocation of housing.

2.2.1.1. Data on homelessness reexamined

On the basis of the analysis of available sources, it is evident that there was never a count of homeless people in the European Union and that country estimates, in the form in which they are presently available, are not comparable. In order to document the extent of homelessness in the European Union on the basis of data and estimates available for the 12 countries, one cannot simply add the crude figures. While it is not possible to advance a specific figure to document, with precision, the magnitude of homelessness, it is possible to make preliminary estimates by adjusting the available data in accordance with a number of hypotheses based on research findings.

Adjustments of country-specific figures based on a number of hypotheses are necessary to achieve the minimum standards of comparability between figures. Our hypothesis will be based on the only available, although somewhat imperfect, tool: analogy. Representative research findings and counts made in some countries will be used as the basis for estimates for countries where similar data are not available. The resulting estimates will not be identical to assessments of the extent of homelessness made for some Member States by their national authorities or by some national researchers.

For the national policy purposes and for the estimates of the level of unmet needs for assistance, we acknowledge that a broader variety of conditions of homelessness may need to be taken into account. National research is needed to estimate the country, and even region specific, fluctuation rates which would enable the scientific community and policy makers to assess, with precision, flows into and out of homelessness. These tasks still stand, as a challenge, before the national research communities and funding agencies.

In order to find the common denominator for the 12 countries, we have adjusted the available figures according to a number of research based hypothesis. Our estimate is based on the magnitude of the population registered as homeless in censuses and surveys, and on the magnitude of the population which has been depending on public and voluntary services for urgent accommodation and housing. Our estimate of the extent of homelessness does not refer only to people sleeping rough and squatting. But, it does not include those homeless people who are not able to access adequate housing but are, however, able to pay for their own precarious accommodation at the margin of the regular rental market. Our initial estimate gives an indication of the average annual number of people who are homeless and who would have been on the streets, had they not been sheltered in urgent accommodation by the public and voluntary services or housed by the local authorities.

In order to estimate the number of homeless people at one point in time in the course of a year, and the number of people who depended on services for shelter over the course of a year, a series of assumptions are made.

2.2.1.2. Hypothesis

The initial estimate of the magnitude of homelessness will not include people in boarding houses and furnished rooms rented on a short-term basis for which they themselves cover the full costs. The estimates will be based only on figures concerning the population dependent on public and voluntary services for accommodation, and on data from censuses and surveys.

We will use official acceptances made by the authorities wherever available as a basis for the estimation of the number of homeless people.

Due to the limited number of shelters available to homeless people and the lack of statutory obligation on authorities to monitor homelessness and housing needs, estimates for Spain, Greece and Portugal will reflect the very low offer of services rather than the magnitude of the population in need of housing assistance. Figures will be subsequently adjusted so as to include people living in extremely sub-standard accommodation which, in other European Union countries, would have been classified as homeless.

The fluctuation rate which gives an indication of the difference in the number of people who are assessed to be homeless at one point in the year and those who are expected to become homeless in the course of a year, as calculated for Germany, will be applied for other countries. The fluctuation rate for Germany is estimated at 38.5 per cent and is based on a comprehensive research of homelessness (Ruhstrat, 1994). Our hypothesis is that the rate is comparable to the fluctuation in other European Union countries.

Where only flow data are available, the stock data will be adjusted by the estimated fluctuation rate in order to assess the number of people who may have been homeless at one point of time in the year.

The average duration of stay in shelters, which is documented as two months for Belgium, will be applied to estimate the extent of homelessness for countries where only data on the turnover in shelters are available.

When applied to available country data the hypotheses are:

Belgium: Data on the turnover in shelters for homeless people and information from shelters on the duration of stay are the basis for the calculation of the average number of sheltered people on one particular day. The fluctuation rate of 38.5 is used to estimate the total number of people who may have depended on shelters over the course of a year. Since both stock and flow data are estimated, figures are rounded up.

Germany: Data provided in the national report based on the projection model are taken over.

Denmark: Data from shelters on the number of people accommodated at one point in time are adjusted according to the fluctuation rate of 38.5 to give an indication of the number of people who may have been homeless over the course of one year.

Spain: The average duration of stay in shelters of two months and the turnover of 38.5 per cent is used to assess the average number of people who were dependant on public and voluntary shelters at one point in time, whilst dependence over the course of one year will be assessed on the basis of available data on the turnover in shelters. Since stock and flow data are estimated, figures are rounded up.

France: The estimation for 1993 based on population census figures gives an indication of the number of homeless people on a particular day. The fluctuation rate of 38.5 per cent is applied to estimate the number of people who may have been homeless over the course of the year.

Greece: Estimates based on personal research of the national corespondent of the Observatory are adjusted by the fluctuation rate of 38.5 per cent to estimate the number of people who may have been homeless in the course of a year.

Ireland: The official estimate made by the local authorities is adjusted by the fluctuation rate of 38.5 to estimate the number of people who may have been homeless over the course of a year.

Italy: Estimates for Italy reflect only the condition of categories of people in extreme poverty on which the Survey of Poverty provided data. Our initial estimate includes only people with no fixed abode and does not take into account immigrants, gypsies and mental patients. An average number of people with no fixed abode estimated in a survey on poverty is adjusted according to the fluctuation rate of 38.5 to estimate the number of people who may have been homeless over the course of a year.

Luxembourg: Data from shelters on the number of people accommodated at one point in time are adjusted according to the fluctuation rate of 38.5 to give an indication of the number of people who may have been homeless over the course of one year.

Netherlands: Only the number of people estimated to be dependent on public and voluntary services, as given in the projection model, are taken into account for our estimation. The homeless population which is living in privately rented rooms and paying for their own accommodation are not included in our estimation. The stock figure is adjusted by the fluctuation rate of 38.5 per cent to estimate the number of people who may have been dependent on services for homeless people over the course of the year.

Portugal: The average duration of stay in shelters of two months was used as the basis for calculating the number of homeless people on an average day on basis of figures on the turnover in shelters. The fluctuation rate of 38.5 per cent was used to estimate the number of people who may have depended on services for homeless people over the course of a year. Since stock and flow data are estimated, figures are rounded up.

United Kingdom: The average household size is used to estimate the number of people who lived in 159,974 households officially accepted for housing by the authorities as homeless or potentially homeless in 1993. In order to estimate the number of people who may have been homeless but were not assessed to be in priority need for housing by the local authorities, the acceptance figure is increased by 20 per cent. The difference of 20 per cent results from the number of people assessed by the local authorities to be homeless and the number of people assessed to be in housing need by the local authorities in Ireland. In Ireland the Housing Act requires that local authorities assess both the number of homeless people and the number of people in housing need. Such data are not available for the United Kingdom. Since official statistics do not diffuse data on the number of people assessed to be homeless or potentially homeless on an average day, we have used the fluctuation rate of 38.5 per cent to estimate the stock from the total number of people who may have been homeless over the one year period.

2.2.1.3. Results

On the basis of the available data and above hypothesis, the minimum number of people every year who depend on public and voluntary services for temporary shelter and housing may be tentatively estimated at 1.8 million (Table 2). On an average day as many as 1.1 million people may have to rely on accommodation provided by the public and voluntary sector, or squat or sleep rough, because they cannot afford a home.

Estimates of the number of homeless people, which would include homeless people in boarding houses and furnished rooms who are paying for their own temporary accommodation or are casually doubling up with friends and relatives, would considerably increase the figures. National experts and organizations working with the homeless suggest that the minimum estimates of the extent of homelessness in the European Union should be increased, on average, by 30 to 50 per cent. This would imply that in the 12 Members States of the European Union between 2.3 million and 2.7 million people may be homeless over the course of the year.

Table 2:   Estimated average annual number of homeless people who may have been dependent on public and voluntary services in the early 1990s

Country	On an average day, or on the day of a survey	Over the course of a year[5]
Belgium	4,000	5,500
Germany	490,700	876,450
Denmark	2,947	4,000
Spain	8,000	11,000
France	250,000	346,000
Greece	5,500	7,700
Ireland	2,667	3,700
Italy	56,000	78,000
Luxembourg	194	200
Netherlands	7,000	12,000
Portugal	3,000	4,000
UK	283,000	460,000

Source: Calculated by the author on the basis of information given in National Reports on Homelessness, when available, and on the basis of personal research.

People who have nowhere to turn to for assistance and are living in shacks, tents, containers or caravans, may be said to be living under extreme housing exclusion, even though they may not be considered as

---

5   Latest available year, see table 1

homeless by the public authorities. In our view, at least 45,000 vagrants and some 100,000 people in extreme housing need in Spain, 60,000 people living in tents, containers or caravans in Greece, at least 70,000 people living in extreme poverty in Italy, close to 90,000 people living in shacks in Portugal, complement the picture of extreme housing exclusion in countries where very few public and voluntary services are available for the homeless and for people in extreme housing need.

When data about homeless people who may have been dependent on public services and people who relied on their private coping strategies under conditions of extreme exclusion from the regular housing market are combined, the figures give a broader image of the extent of homelessness in southern Member States. They bring the minimum estimate of the number of people excluded from decent housing who, in most other Member States, would be considered as homeless, to at least 160,000 people in Spain, as many as 67,000 in Greece, to 150,000 in Italy and close to 100,000 in Portugal.

2.2.2. Trends in homelessness and socio-demographic characteristics of homeless people assisted by the public and voluntary sector

Organizations working with the homeless have been reporting a growing number of people seeking assistance in the 1980s and early 1990s because they do not have a dwelling. In England and Wales, the index of increase in the number of those officially recognized by the authorities as homeless and potentially homeless is 280 for the 1978/1992 period (1978 was the year when data were first collected). As noted before, the number of homeless households which have been accepted for housing in England and Wales has declined in 1993. The index of growth between 1978 and 1993 for the United Kingdom as a whole was 258. In Flanders the index of growth in the number of people who passed through shelters for 1988/1992 was 120. In the Netherlands the number of homeless people is expected to increase to 53 thousand by the end of the 1990s (Heydendael et al., 1990). The index of growth for the 1989/1994 period was close to 140. The average annual growth in the number of homeless people who were sheltered and rehoused ranged between 5 per cent in Flanders, and 8 per cent in the Netherlands at the lower end of the scale, and 16 per cent in Luxembourg and in the United Kingdom at the upper end.

If the tendencies observed during recent years persist in the 12 Member States, the number of homeless people who have exhausted their private networks and individual coping strategies and may become dependent on the public and voluntary services, could reach 6.6 million by the turn of the century.

A survey undertaken in France showed that 47 per cent of service providers estimated the current supply of short-term accommodation to be insufficient in number, and 55 per cent stressed the shortage of shelters providing medium duration accommodation (FNARS, 1994). The only country where shelters are not full to the maximum of their capacity throughout the year is Denmark, though even in this country it is not unusual for shelters to be overcrowded in winter time. Elsewhere, service providers report an increasing pressure on shelters, both in terms of the number of people and the duration of stay. Demand for permanent housing is largely unmet. In England and Wales only four out of 10 households who apply for housing as homeless are accepted for housing by the local authorities.

Thus, it may not be possible to estimate the exact extent of homelessness for each year, but information from public and voluntary service providers points towards the conclusion that the number of extremely poor people who cannot afford a decent dwelling and who could no longer rely on private networks has been increasing throughout the early 1990s. Traditional safety nets formed by relatives and friends are no longer an efficient insurance against homelessness. Not only is the number of people who turn to the public and voluntary sector for shelter and housing assistance growing, but also the composition of the homeless population who turns to services for homeless people is changing.

2.2.2.1. Women in sheltered accommodation

The share of women who lose their home probably does not differ much from that of men (Renard and Van Menxel, 1993). Traditionally, what did distinguish homeless men and homeless women were their coping strategies. When excluded from housing, men turned to social and voluntary organizations in far greater numbers than women. Throughout the second half of the 1980s, 7-8 out of 10 single sheltered people in the European Union countries were men. This could be interpreted by two tentative conclusions: firstly, men were less inclined to maintain family and establish lasting relations and informal networks on which they could rely at times of existential crisis; and secondly, the public and the voluntary sectors have been building services around the premise of diverging male and female coping strategies. The offer of shelters for single women has traditionally been very low and is generally estimated among organisations working with the homeless in the European Union as insufficient.

The overwhelming prevalence of men among single homeless who turned to shelters started gradually changing in the late 1980s and has gained pace in the early 1990s. Typically, in 1993 four out of 10 sheltered people were women. All European Union countries are reporting an increase in the number of women seeking assistance because they have no home (FEANTSA, 1993).

By way of example, in Denmark the proportion of women among the sheltered population increased from 6 per cent to 20 per cent between 1976 and 1989. Particularly vulnerable are lone mothers in need of emergency accommodation. Indeed, half of the sheltered women in Denmark had children with them (Salicath and Thomson, 1992). The share of women among people sheltered as homeless in Belgium reached almost 40 per cent in 1993. Half of sheltered women had children with them. Twice as many sheltered women as men were below the age of 18. Almost four out of 10 sheltered women were below the age of 25, three out of 10 men were below 25 years of age (Amascopie, 1993; Thuislozenzorg, 1993). A one day census among service providers in Luxembourg showed that 41 per cent of the homeless population in shelters were women. FNARS, which gathers 700 French associations and organizations and 1,600 centres and services for homeless people and which has provided accommodation for 34,000 homeless people (FNARS, 1995), signals an increase in the number of homeless women, sheltered either alone or with a partner or a child.

Data from hostels for single homeless people in England show that, on average, one in four residents were women. However, in the younger age groups, below the age of 25, homeless women were disproportionably represented. Among sheltered residents below the age of 18 more than half, i.e. 55 per cent were women (Randall, 1992). Moreover, 40 per cent of London hostel residents were women, and women were disproportionately represented in the under 25 years old, i.e. women represented 66 per cent of the 25 years old group (SHiL, 1992).

We have no data to assess changes in the level of domestic violence over time. What seems to stem from research on homelessness is that women may be becoming less prone to tolerate domestic abuse. Although there are no national statistics on the number of women who become homeless because they are escaping from sexual abuse and violence, a survey in 12 hostels in England found that four in 10 homeless women reported that they became homeless as a result of sexual and/or physical abuse (Hendessi, 1993).

Public authorities in the United Kingdom do not publish data on the demographic characteristics of households accepted for housing as homeless. However, due to the fact that eight out of 10 households accepted for rehousing in the United Kingdom are families with dependent children, it may be said that women account for at least as many rehoused persons as men. An estimate for England indicates that 6-8 out of 10 homeless applicants for rehousing were women (Ashcroft, 1993).

2.2.2.2. *Age, education and employment record of sheltered people*

The majority of roofless people in the European Union countries are at their prime working age. More than half of sheltered people are between 20 and 39 years of age. This age group accounts for 30.5 per cent of the total population of the European Union (EUROSTAT, 1992) and for 55 per cent of the homeless population (FEANTSA, 1993).

The stunning characteristic of homelessness in 1993 and 1994 is the growth in the number of young adults who turn to shelters for homeless people for accommodation. In less than a year, the number of demands for shelter by youngsters aged 18 to 25 was estimated by the voluntary service providers in France to have increased substantially. During the winter 1993/1994 in the Centre d'Action Sociale Protestant which shelters some 120 people on daily basis, one in four homeless people were in the 18 to 25 age group. One third of sheltered homeless people in Belgium are below the age of 25. One out of 10 is below the age of 18. Evidence from Ireland also highlights an increase in the rate of youth homelessness. Furthermore, the lack of suitable accommodation for children who become homeless, and the increase in the length of stay in bed and breakfast accommodation is reported both by researchers and service providers in Ireland. The age of children placed in bed and breakfast accommodation for homeless children, under section 5 of the Child Care Act, varied between 13 and 18. In 1991 the average length of stay for homeless children in bed and breakfast was 11.6 nights, by 1993 it increased to 35.1 nights (O'Sullivan, 1994).

The majority of sheltered homeless people have low educational attainment. In Belgium one out of two sheltered people has dropped out of school during primary, or immediately after completing elementary, education. In Germany eight out of 10, in Luxembourg nine out of 10 sheltered people have only primary education or no schooling.

Among people in emergency shelters the majority are jobless, or have had casual, unstable jobs of short duration. The share of homeless who earned an income from their work at the time of admittance, or shortly before entering a shelter, ranges between 5 per cent in Germany at the lower end of the scale, and 15 per cent in Belgium, at the upper end of the scale (Renard and Van Menxel, 1993). However, the vast majority of homeless people have worked at some point in their life, and those who have never worked constitute a small minority. Typically, 8-9 out of 10 homeless people have had a professional experience (FEANTSA, 1993).

2.2.2.3. Relational situation of people in sheltered accommodation

The most striking feature of the sheltered population, when compared to others, is the very high proportion of single people. In the age group 20 to 40 nine out of 10 homeless men, and six out of 10 homeless women have no partner. When they have a home, eight out of 10 men and nine out of 10 women form a couple (Corijn, 1993; Matthiesen, 1988). Typically, out of 10 sheltered men, seven are single and two are separated or divorced. Among homeless women, three out of 10 are single, four are married and three are separated or divorced. The prevalence of divorce among homeless people, particularly women, suggests that for the underprivileged social groups marital breakdown may be a factor precipitating homelessness.

The magnitude of solitude among rough-sleepers and sheltered people which emerges from small-scale interviews in the European Union countries (McCarthy, 1988; Nuy 1993) and stories told by homeless people (Filosa, 1993; Laussinotte, 1994) is manifested at aggregate level through data collected in shelters. The incidence of single people who do not have a lasting relationship needs to be viewed within the context of personality characteristics, defective primary socialization and failure of the public institutions to assist children and young adults from under-privileged families who have psychological and social handicaps.

Among homeless women the incidence of marriage, divorce and sepa-ration is higher than among homeless men, suggesting that marital breakdown, whether *de facto* or *de jure*, frequently precedes or coincides with homelessness. By contrast, the incidence of men who have never been married among the homeless may imply that their formative experience within the family of origin and their current social exclusion mark their propensity to live alone. Indeed, the overwhelming majority of sheltered men have never been married.

Among those people with no accommodation who are sheltered as single homeless people, the overwhelming majority do not have lasting rela-tionships with the other gender. When data on cohabitation are available, the share of sheltered people who have a permanent intimate relationship is marginal. The share of people without a fixed abode who declared in an Italian survey to have a cohabitant stood at 6 out of 100 inter-viewed (Tosi and Ranci, 1993).

2.2.2.4. Nationality

On average, most people in sheltered accommodation are nationals of the country in which they are homeless and typically, between eight and nine people out of 10 staying in urgent accommodation belong to autochthon population groups. The sheltered homeless non-EU immi-grants constitute only a fraction of homeless people. Their educational attainment is generally higher than that of sheltered nationals and this may imply that their condition might not be as durable as for other homeless people who have no qualifications. However, homeless immi-grants may be more visible due to their phenotypic features and lack of fluency in the language of the host country. Indeed in countries where a high pressure of illegal immigration is recorded, namely in Spain, Italy and Greece, homelessness is frequently perceived by the general public as a phenomenon affecting principally immigrants.

The impact of immigration on housing exclusion, more particularly in countries which have received high numbers of immigrants in the early 1990s, can be measured in terms of the demographic pressure on the available housing stock, rather than by figures from service providers for homeless people. Immigrants of German origin, "Aussiedler", living in transitory homes in Germany, repatriates from Pontos in Greece or asylum seekers in other European Union countries are sheltered under conditions defined by international law and immigration legislation and policies of host countries. Housing needs which result from ethnically selective immigration policy, and accommodation arrangements provided by governments to displaced persons and asylum seekers, need to be addressed in a study in its own right. The key questions related to living conditions of these categories of immigrants to be answered are how transitory and how adequate the temporary accommodation provided by the authorities is.

Likewise, housing conditions of illegal immigrants cannot be documented on the basis of available data from service providers for homeless people. Shelters for homeless people are not allowed to accommodate illegal immigrants. Thus, while immigrants may not be exerting pressure on shelters, their living conditions need to be perceived both in terms of the quality of their accommodation, and the price of the marginal housing sector which they can access. For paperless immigrants low-quality, usually high-price, housing at the margin of the rental market is the only option. The impact on the marginal rental market can be ambiguous. On the one hand, a large presence of illegal immigrants may be favouring housing speculation. On the other hand, it may also be contributing to pulling out of poverty of very low-income groups in the autochthon population who are renting, usually illegally, parts of their dwellings.

2.2.2.5. Health status

As may be expected, the health status of the sheltered population is hazardous. Both physical and mental problems associated with their living conditions and access (if any) only to primary health care, result in high incidence of diseases typically associated with poverty. Malnutrition and diseases related to bad diets, lasting solitude, insecurity of temporary night shelters, all inevitably affect the health status and longevity of homeless people. However, transnational comparisons are impossible to make due to fragmentary research and above all biased sampling. Shelters that do not admit drug addicts will record a different health profile of homeless people from shelters in Denmark. In Denmark generous social policy plays an important role in preventing homelessness which may result from income insufficiency. Thus, people who fall through social safety nets will become homeless due to individual traumatic events or personality characteristics, rather than primary poverty. Indeed, data from shelters signal the prevalence of people with alcohol and drug dependence. Six out of 10 sheltered Danes had a substance abuse problem (FEANTSA, 1993).

Two health surveys may illustrate the extreme variety of health profiles of homeless. In a Brussels project (Médecins sans Frontières, 1993) aimed at offering health care to people sleeping rough, two out of 10 treated had respiratory problems, mainly pneumonia, two were treated for dermatological problems, one each for cardiological, and digestive disorders, one for psychiatric problems and one for problems related to drug addiction.

Some aspects of the health status of homeless people which may be considered as menacing for the population as a whole, gain particular public attention. Typically, it is the incidence of infectious diseases which raises public concern. During the winter of 1993, 250 men and women in shelters in London were screened by doctors for tuberculosis. Four active cases were found (CRISIS, 1994). The press reported that a possible incidence of TB in two per cent of the sheltered population in London was "a figure worse than the Third World" (The Independent, 9 March 1994).

Focusing solely on the health status of those homeless people sleeping rough and in shelters for homeless people results in underestimating the magnitude of exclusion from adequate housing, and in stigmatization of people who share the condition of homelessness. Frequently, personal problems, mental illness and substance abuse as determinants of homelessness are overestimated. While deinstitutionalization of mental care, which has not been compensated for by the development of community base care, has undeniably added discharged psychiatric patients to the homeless population, the majority of sheltered individuals with stress symptoms have no institutional history. The information that 18 per cent of the sheltered in Madrid in 1991 had mental health problems, or that 53 per cent of the homeless surveyed in 1992 in Portugal had mental health problems needs to be taken *cum grano di salis*. When the level of poverty in a country is high and the available services for the needy are few, only extremely destitute people will be assisted, usually by charitable organizations.

When the number of homeless people assisted by the public and voluntary services is very low due to a low supply of services, as is the case in some southern Member States, or is low due to an efficient preventive policy, as is the case in some northern member States, the effect of population assortment can be clearly observed. When the numbers are low, personality characteristics and chance events, on the one hand, and the organizational set up of services, on the other, determine the profile of users.

Furthermore, available data about mental health problems of homeless people which are not gathered on a systematic basis lack an essential information. We do not know when symptoms of mental disorders first occurred. Being an alcoholic when homeless is qualitatively different from becoming an alcoholic once homeless. When a battered woman escapes family violence and becomes homeless, the state of her mental health will be shattered, but it will usually be a consequence of the trauma reinforced by a loss of a home and not a cause of the condition of homelessness.

2.3. BADLY HOUSED PEOPLE

From an anthropological perspective, housing is both a basic need and a prerequisite for the satisfaction of other basic and more complex psychological and cultural needs. Needs for security, independence, privacy, education, self-development, leisure and social interaction are associated to the safety of a home. Available space and adequacy of a dwelling may provide a favourable environment, but, may also delimit the condition of housing stress which will make the development of one or more human potentials impossible. Housing stress defines the degree of housing exclusion and may operate as impetus to marginalization of individuals who become more vulnerable to extreme social exclusion and homelessness. Experience of overcrowding and housing insecurity in the family of origin, together with other manifest forms of poverty, may trace the path to social exclusion for young adults. Bad housing may also be linked to poor health, safety hazards, higher exposure to the elements.

Key housing indicators of adequacy may include a varying number of items defining quantity and price, quality in terms of structure and density, and tenure (e.g. Priemus, 1992). While acknowledging the necessity to perceive the complexity of criteria defining adequate housing, our analysis is, *a priori*, limited by the limiting nature of available data. Available data on housing conditions in the 12 Members States enable us to document only three indicators of exclusion from adequate housing; dwellings which have no inside sanitary facilities, overcrowded, and sub-standard dwellings.

Using sanitary facilities as an indicator of housing inadequacy does not imply that we consider all the people living in dwellings without indoor sanitary facilities to be under housing stress. Indeed, in Belgium, a wing added to the old building will frequently include sanitary facilities and a kitchen which may be accessible only via the garden. These old houses may be built in solid material, may be spacious and otherwise adequate. This condition will differ profoundly from that of people living in cities and having to share a common toilet or a bathroom with other tenants. On the other hand, in the United Kingdom the proportion of households registered as having no direct access to sanitary facilities is just one per cent (Tables 4 and 5). Yet, there are as many as 3.5 million properties in need of major repairs (Department of Environment, 1993). The state of disrepair is clearly a more appropriate indicator to identify bad housing conditions in the United Kingdom.

Elementary sanitary infrastructure is just one in the line of indicators of the condition of bad housing. Detailed analysis of living conditions of people would further enable us to identify, with precision, the proportion of inadequately housed people who may be considered to be in housing stress. Such analysis imminently has to be based on a country-specific approach which will take into account not only economic factors but also cultural ones, the climate, type of settlements, habitat.

Likewise, overcrowding may be defined in country-specific terms, measured against possibilities, norms and preferences of people living in a multitude of household forms, with sex and age composition of its members as important variables. National averages and transnational comparisons may be deceiving. The socio-psychological literature

102

suggests different minimum thresholds of available space. The threshold below which limited space can have a pathological impact on the psycho-physical development was identified at between 8-10 square meters per household member (de Lauwe, 1960). The critical threshold below which tensions within the family are likely to be frequent was established by the same author at 12-14 square meters. However, available space does not operate as an independent factor of housing stress and its impact is determined in conjunction with other structural features. The number of persons per room and the structure of the dwellings are stressed by numerous authors as indicators which may play a more important role in determining overcrowding than the actual surface of a dwelling (Epstein, 1988; Knowles, 1979; Parke and Sawin, 1979; Booth and Edwards, 1976).

Setting standards for minimum space imminently implies simplifying the multitude of human conditions and reducing them to averages. However, we need to identify indicators as a starting point for the analysis which may help us to identify the population sub-group that cannot afford an adequate dwelling. Like any other effort to document a social condition by resorting to national statistics, this one calls for caution, particularly in making transnational comparisons. The legal systems and social policy aims may be converging in the European Union (Walker, 1994), but the historical dimension of social and cultural reality is still deeply rooted in the social fabric of each country. The same indicators of adequate housing do not necessarily have the same relevance for all the countries. In some countries sanitary facilities added to the main building to which there is no direct access from the main dwelling, or adjacent constructions, will be classified as dwellings without inside facilities. In others they will be considered as inside facilities with perfectly adequate access. In some countries it may be expected that a person living alone should have at least two rooms. Elsewhere, one person per room might be too high a standard.

Even when criteria defining a condition may be uniform, the statistical information is not always standardised and the tabulation systems may vary from one country to another. Difficulties in documenting the quality of dwellings in a transnational perspective may be typically illustrated by the lack of any definition of good housing, basic comfort or sub-standard accommodation in the Statistics on Housing in the European Union (Commission of the European Communities, 1993a). However, while acknowledging limitations, it may be argued that information about the state of the housing stock in the European Union countries provided by the national statistical offices may be a useful tool. This could serve two purposes: putting the phenomenon of inadequate housing in an international perspective, and documenting the historical evolution of housing conditions.

2.3.1. People in dwellings without inside sanitary facilities

For the initial assessment of the magnitude of the population excluded from adequate housing we will use one minimum standard of adequacy: (no) access to sanitary infrastructure. The minimum sanitary infrastructure consists of an inside water closet, and bath or a shower. If this minimum criterion is not met we can identify a condition of potential dwelling inadequacy. National classifications of dwellings according to access to sanitary infrastructure will be used.

Available data on households which do not have an inside toilet (Table 3) point toward two conclusions: firstly, that a high number of citizens of the European Union lived in the late 1980s in dwellings in which they did not have elementary sanitary infrastructure, and secondly, that countries exhibit profound differences. The share of households without inside WC ranged between 0 per cent in the Netherlands and 44 per cent in Portugal.

Three European Union countries, The Netherlands, Luxembourg and the United Kingdom, had below one per cent of households without an inside toilet. Germany, Italy and Denmark registered between one and five percent, Ireland, Spain and France between five and 10 percent, Belgium and Greece between 10 and 15 percent. Portugal stood out with the highest share of households which did not have an inside WC, almost one in two households (44 percent).

Although in the majority of countries the share of households without the very basic sanitary installation was below 10 percent, the number of people living in such dwellings can by no way be considered as marginal. Indeed, in France, for example, more than 5 million people did not have a WC in their dwelling. In the 12 European Union countries, on average, 5.5 per cent of the total population lived in the second half of 1980s in dwellings without an elementary sanitary amenity. This relatively small share accounted for 20 million people who had no access to a WC in their own dwelling.

Table 3: **Households without elementary sanitary infrastructure around 1985**

	No inside WC		
	Households		People *
	percent	number	
Belgium	13.1	517,843	1,398,176
Denmark	3.0	67,530	148,566
Germany	1.6	557,232	1,337,357
Greece	15.4	514,976	1,596,425
Spain	8.0	963,200	3,467,520
France	9.5	2,045,825	5,523,727
Ireland	6.1	62,769	219,691
Italy	1.9	392,274	1,176,822
Luxembourg	0.5	725	2,102
Netherlands	0	0	0
Portugal	44.0	1,397,440	4,611,552
UK	0.9	205,200	533,520
TOTAL EU		6,725,014	20,015,458

Source: Calculated by the author on the basis of data from EUROSTAT, 1992

* Estimation made on the basis of the number of households and average household size in the year of observation.

The distribution of countries according to the accessibility of the very basic sanitary facility in private dwellings corresponds neither to the level of overall development measured by the Gross National Product (GNP), GNP per household, the share of the population living below the poverty line, nor to the standard of living measured by indicators such as average earnings, social benefits, household consumption and health. Belgium, for example had the lowest share of the population living below the poverty line (EUROSTAT, 1990) and a generous social policy, but the share of households without the most basic sanitary utility was high by European Union standards. Indeed, the share of households without an inside WC was threefold higher than the share of the population living below the poverty line. By contrast, in Italy the share of households without a WC was tenfold lower than the share of poor households. This ambiguity may be largely ascribed to differences in how rigorously outdoor access or shared facilities were classified in the two countries. Clearly, standards of adequacy used by the national statistical offices are by no means uniform and may be considerably higher in some European Union countries. This seems to have been the case for Belgium.

Table 4: Households without basic sanitary infrastructure around 1985

| | No inside bathroom or shower room | | |
| | Households | | People * |
	percent	number	number
Belgium	20.1	794,553	2,145,293
Denmark	6.0	135,060	297,132
Germany	4.8	1,671,696	4,012,070
Greece	15.6	521.664	1,617,158
Spain	17.0	2,046,800	7,368,480
France	8.0	1,722,800	4,651,560
Ireland	8.2	84,378	295,323
Italy	6.9	1,424,570	4,273,710
Luxembourg	2.5	3,625	10,512
Netherlands	2.1	128,835	347,854
Portugal	44.0	1,397,440	4,611,552
UK	1.0	228,000	592,800
TOTAL EU		10,159,385	30,223,444

Source: Calculated by the author on the basis of data from EUROSTAT, 1992

* Estimation made on the basis of the number of households and average household size in the year of observation.

A similar conclusion, but based on higher shares of people excluded from adequate housing, may be drawn from data on dwellings which did not have a bathroom or a shower room (Table 4). Thirty million Union citizens could not afford the comfort of a bathroom or a shower room in their dwelling.

The share of households without this basic sanitary infrastructure ranged between one per cent in the United Kingdom, at the lower end of the scale, and 44 per cent in Portugal, at the upper end of the scale. Countries fell into five groups: less than one per cent, United Kingdom; between one and five percent, the Netherlands and Luxembourg; between five and 10 per cent, Germany, Denmark, Italy, France and Ireland; between 10 and 20 per cent, Greece, Spain and Belgium; 44 per cent, Portugal.

The latest available data for all the 12 countries are those for the second half of the 1980s. More recent data would no doubt show a decrease in the number of dwellings without basic sanitary facilities. However, they have become available only in some European Union countries and are not strictly comparable. By way of example, a survey of occupied dwellings in Italy (ISTAT, 1993), as opposed to the above data for all dwellings, registered only 2.1 per cent of households as having no bathroom in 1991. The survey reported that 79 per cent of occupied dwellings possessed all basic amenities: running water, inside toilet, electric supply, bathroom, hot water and heating.

2.3.2. People in overcrowded and sub-standard dwellings

The impact of cultural norms and housing realities delimits the relative nature of minimum standards of space and quality of dwellings needed to meet the household needs. The mosaic created by data documenting country-specific criteria seems to be more appropriate for the illustration of overcrowding than the imposition of uniform standards. We will thus give estimates based on national standards as proposed by the national experts.

Belgium: Renard (1994) proposes as a basis for evaluating whether dwellings are appropriate in terms of size, the standard of one room per person for multi person households, and 2 rooms for a single person. According to this criteria, some 245,000 households or 6.2 per cent of all households do not dispose of such space. The total number of people living in dwellings which are below optimal standards of space as defined above, amounts to 10.7 per cent of the total population, or over one million people.

Marginal housing in camping and furnished rooms seems to cause major public concern. However, due to the lack of data, the extent of marginal housing could not be documented.

Denmark: In 1985, average number of occupants per room was 0.6. Thus, overcrowding does not affect the population as a whole. However, in 1991 two per cent of households disposed of one room for two or more persons, which implies that the number of people living under conditions of marked overcrowding can be estimated at just above 100,000. In addition, in 9 per cent of households, one to two people lived in one room. This figure implies that close to one million people live under conditions of relative overcrowding.

Sub-standard housing seems not to be a problem. Very few people live in marginal accommodation as urban renovation has practically eliminated condemned housing. Untraditional ways of living in small houses surrounded by vegetable gardens seem to reflect individual preference of some groups (Rostgaard and Koch-Nielsen, 1994).

Germany: The threshold for the estimation of the extent of overcrowding is defined by the condition when the number of people exceeds by two, each of the number of rooms in a dwelling. A total of 192,130 overcrowded units (Ruhstrat and Busch-Geertsema, 1994) were estimated in 1987 in West Germany alone. This means that some 1,150,000 people lived in units which did not meet the minimum space requirements.

Spain: More than two people sharing a room is the criteria for overcrowding proposed by Salinas Ramos (1994). In 1991 the share of households living in overcrowded dwellings stood at 14.4 percent. Between 1981 and 1991 overcrowding remained unchanged for households with 4 members and even increased for three member households. The share of households implies that some 5.5 million people live in overcrowded dwellings.

France: The criteria combining quality of dwellings and available space used in a housing survey by the National Statistical Office (INSEE) put forward the figure of 10.6 per cent of badly housed households in 1988. This implies that some 6 million people were housed in overcrowded and sub-standard dwellings.

Préel (1992) suggested the figure of 1,576,000 people who live in mobile or sub-standard dwellings.

Greece: Estimates can be made only about the extremely marginalized population since data from the 1991 census have not been made available. People living in tents, caravans, containers and alike are estimated by Sapounakis (1994) at 60,000. Living conditions of these people may be said to be closer to homelessness than bad housing.

Ireland: The assessment of housing needs which local authorities conduct every two years, estimates the number of households living in overcrowded conditions in 1993 at 7,075 households. Those living in unfit or materially unsuitable accommodation were estimated at 5,122. Other categories include households unable to afford existing accommodation, involuntarily sharing accommodation, the elderly, the homeless, those in need of accommodation for medical/compassionate reasons, travellers, disabled/handicapped persons, and young persons leaving institutional care or without family accommodation. The total number of households in housing need was estimated at 28,624. The number of people assessed to be in housing need was 82,886 (Housing Statistics Bulletin, 1993).

The figure for 1993 shows an increase of almost 20 per cent in the number of households in housing need in comparison to 1991. Over the two year period the highest increase may be observed for the group unable to afford existing accommodation.

Italy: The criteria adopted by the National statistical office (ISTAT, 1993) define two sub-groups in overcrowded dwellings. Serious overcrowding is defined as more than 1.6 persons per room, less serious as more than 1.2 persons per room. The central area consists of an average occupation density of between 1.2 and 0.8 persons per room (Tosi and Ranci, 1994). Overcrowding decreased substantially between 1975 and 1991. The share of people living under severe crowding fell from 9.6 in 1975 to 3.3 in 1991. Over the same period less serious overcrowding decreased from 37.7 per cent of all households to 8.0 per cent. This implies that the number of people affected by serious overcrowding may be estimated at some 680,000 people, and moderate overcrowding at 4.4 million people.

The share of the population living in sub-standard dwellings without essential amenities decreased substantially between 1981 and 1991. The share of occupied dwellings without one of the amenities, running water, toilet, electric supply, bathroom, hot water and heating, fell to 21 per cent for the country as a whole. In the North the share is half of the national average and stands at 11 per cent of all households. Tosi and Ranci (1994) estimate that 2 per cent of households live under acute housing hardship without essential indispensable amenities, WC, bath or shower and hot water. This amounts to more than 400,000 families or over one million people. Slight hardship due to the lack or insufficiency of basic amenities is estimated to affect 10 per cent, i.e. more than two million households in which as many as 5.8 million people live.

The population census classified 45,000 units as "other type of dwellings" which basically include basements, garrets, warehouses or permanently occupied caravans. An estimate of the number of badly housed people based on criteria of economic poverty and bad housing conditions in terms of unfitness and unsuitability for habitation (Caritas-Irs, 1994) identified 600,000 households with about 1.7-1.8 million people paying very high rents. At least a quarter of poor owner-occupiers were badly housed, about 300,000 households and 850,000 people. A badly housed threshold below which housing costs were excessive implied that 900,000 households and 2.6 million people were below the threshold (Tosi, 1994).

For people living in unfit accommodation, a "hard core" of badly housed people was estimated at 900,000 households. As a result, Tosi (1994) concludes that the serious housing hardship can be cautiously estimated to affect 4.5 percent of the total population or 2.5 million people.

Luxembourg: The population census data on the state of the housing stock classified 11 per cent of dwellings as having no basic comfort and 9 per cent of dwellings as not being fully equipped. This would imply that almost 27,000 dwellings providing accommodation to some 70,000 people did not meet standards of high quality.

Netherlands: The housing stock is relatively new which implies that the quality of the stock is high. In the mid-1980s only 4 per cent of the housing stock was seriously run down (Commission of the European

Communities, 1993a). This means that some 215,000 dilapidated dwellings provided accommodation for approximately 550,000 people. In recent years, most old houses have been refurbished under national and local government urban renewal programs (de Feijter and Radstaak, 1994). This explains the very low level of sub-standard housing in the country. Today, financial difficulties in maintaining a dwelling are identified as a major source of housing stress.

Portugal: 28,150 households lived in 27,642 shacks and other unconventional dwellings such as caves and staircases and mobile dwellings (INE, Census 1991). If average household size is used as a base for estimates then close to 90,000 people are extremely badly housed. However, this population may be said to be living under conditions which are closer to homelessness than to bad housing. Estimates by the statistical office (Commission of the European Communities, 1993a) about the share of households without basic comfort and amenities and condemned housing amounted to 23 per cent of all dwellings. This means that almost one million dwellings provided bad housing for three million people.

United Kingdom: The bedroom standard is usually used to measure adequacy of the space and overcrowding of dwellings in England and Wales. The English House Condition Survey found that 19,1 million household required some 32 million bedrooms. Using this standard it is estimated that just under 3 per cent or 517,000 households are overcrowded (Carlisle, 1994). This implies that 1.3 million people live in overcrowded dwellings. The extent of overcrowding in Scotland was measured in 1991 (General Register Office, 1993). Out of just more than 2 million households, 72,288 have over one person per room. Of these, 11,352 have over 1.5 persons per room (Aldridge, 1994). This means that some 360,000 people are living in dwellings where there were more than one person per room, while severe overcrowding affected some 57,000 people.

One in thirteen homes in England and Wales is officially unfit (Department of Environment, 1993). Eleven reasons for disrepair were classified and 1,456,000 homes in England and 71,700 homes in Wales were estimated to be unfit. This might be said to constitute the outer core of housing exclusion which may affect as many as 3,6 million people. The 97,000 dwellings found unfit on six or more items which may house some 240,000 people constitute the inner core of bad housing. The House Condition Survey in Scotland (1991) found that 4.7 per cent of Scotland's housing was below the tolerable standard. This amounted to 95,000 dwellings implying that some 240,000 people live in very bad conditions. Humidity was found in an additional 13.2 per cent of the housing stock , i.e. 267,000 dwellings affecting as many as 660,000 people.

We will use minimum standards to identify people under severe housing stress, and not optimal criteria of space and quality of dwellings. People living under conditions of critical overcrowding, with more than two people sharing one room, and people living in dwellings unfit on several items, are living under severe housing stress and are those who constitute the outer core of housing exclusion. It may be estimated that severe housing stress affects at least 15 million people living in severe overcrowding and sub-standard accommodation in the 12 European Union countries. Twice as many, or 30 million people, may not be able to enjoy the comfort of a shower or a bathroom in their dwelling.

2.3.3. People excluded from good housing and well housed people

Introducing additional indicators of the quality of dwellings, in order to assess the magnitude of the population that cannot afford a well-equipped, dry and sufficiently spacious home, will no doubt increase the number of inadequately housed people.

The magnitude of the population that is not necessarily exposed to housing stress, but is nevertheless excluded from good quality housing, may be said to be at the margin of exclusion from adequate housing. This condition may be illustrated by data on the quality of the housing stock as assessed by the governments' statistical agencies. When country- specific indicators of good dwellings are taken as the basis for the estimation of the number of people excluded from quality dwellings in each country, the figures increase dramatically.

Housing Statistics published by the Commission of the European Communities (1993a) which include data on the state of the housing stock, enable us to identify that at least 70 million people in 10 European Union countries (data not available for Germany and Greece) are excluded from dwellings which meet criteria of good quality set-out by the national authorities (Table 5). The publication does not give an explanation of standards of quality and disrepair.

Table 5: **State of the housing stock and people excluded from good quality dwellings in 1991**

	Good dwellings*	Dwellings which do not meet national criteria of good quality***	
	Percentage of the housing stock	Dwellings	People
		Number	
Belgium	57	1,049,440	2,623,600
Denmark	87	308,750	648,375
Spain	49	6,861,720	15,781,956
France	81**	2,361,330	6,139,458
Ireland	87**	135,070	472,745
Italy	52	11,383,680	31,874,304
Luxembourg	80	26,940	75,432
Netherlands	80	1,193,000	3,101,800
Portugal	77	961,653	2,307,967
UK	86	3,325,000	8,312,500
TOTAL		27,606,583	71,338,137

Source : * Commission of the European Communities, 1993a
** Estimated by the author on the basis of the share of dwellings without basic comfort
*** Estimated by the author on the basis of the total number of dwellings, average number of persons per dwelling in the year of observation, and the number of dwellings which were not classified by the national statistical offices as good dwellings

Due to the lack of a theoretical framework and the lack of criteria for defining conditions and standards of adequacy, the analytical value of figures is limited. Indeed, ambiguities of published data are multiple. One can express serious doubts as to the validity of any transnational comparison that would be made on the basis of the information on the percentage of the housing stock assessed as good dwellings. However, the point that we wanted to make is that minimum standards of adequacy form a borderline separating people under severe housing stress from other badly housed people, but that the threshold of quality separates people excluded from good housing from well housed people.

2.4. THE EXTENT OF HOMELESSNESS AND SEVERE HOUSING STRESS

On an average day 1.1 million citizens of the European Union may be dependent on the public and voluntary services for homeless people because they cannot afford accommodation from their own resources. Over the course of a year 1.8 million people may have been dependent on the public and voluntary sector. It may be estimated that as many as 2.7 million people pendulate between public and voluntary services and privately rented rooms at the margin of the rental market or double up with friends and relatives. This population constitutes the inner core of housing exclusion.

The outer core of housing exclusion can be identified on the basis of data documenting conditions of severe housing stress. People living in critically overcrowded and severely sub-standard dwellings are those excluded from adequate dwellings. When minimum standards of adequacy are applied to illustrate the threshold of housing exclusion, they show that some 15 million citizens of the European Union are living under severe housing stress.

Our estimates show that close to 18 million European Union citizens are homeless or extremely badly housed. This figure includes 1.8 million people dependent on services for homeless people, 0.9 million people in privately rented rooms and 15 million people living under severe housing stress. This may be considered as the minimum estimate of the number of people who cannot access adequate housing from their own resources.

The tendency observed between mid-1980s and mid-1990s is that of a growing number of homeless people who turn to public and voluntary shelters and services for accommodation. Among the sheltered and assisted homeless population, lone women and women with a child, and young adults below the age of 25 are the fastest growing homeless population. On the basis of available data it is not possible to determine the average duration of the condition of homelessness. Due to the welfare policies in the Member States, few people are homeless all their adult life. The fact that for the majority of people who lose a home homeless is a transitory state does not make it less important. Homelessness increasingly occurs at the vulnerable moment in the life cycle when the passage into adulthood and parenthood coincides with the breakdown of family solidarity and lack of social opportunity.

Homelessness, as a condition of extreme housing exclusion, may be said to be transitory for the majority of homeless people. But, as a social process of exclusion from housing of a large segment of the population, homelessness and housing stress are a constant. They are a structurally induced feature of the European society at the turn of the 21st century.

According to our knowledge, no comprehensive research about severe housing stress of badly housed people has been undertaken at the European level. Thus, a tentative answer to the question who are badly housed people, can be based only on the contextual data. Determinants of housing exclusion provide such background information and will be addressed in the next chapter.

Chapter 3

SOCIAL CONTEXT
OF HOUSING EXCLUSION

Homelessness as a condition affects individuals. Their condition may be perceived as a consequence of a number of unfortunate circumstances, traumatic events and above all bad choices. But, individuals do not make choices in a social vacuum. The question is not whether a choice is being made. Every aspect of human behaviour may be observed through the sequence of choices. Indeed, homeless people may prefer to sleep rough rather than in a charitable shelter. But, what can be the scope of the rational choice theory approach in the analysis of poverty and housing exclusion? In order to gain insight into opportunities and mechanisms of individual choices the first question to be answered is: from what range of available options can an individual choose? The available options stem from the social processes which occur against a background of structural features. Housing exclusion which affects the homeless and badly housed people operates as a social process through a social context which may delimit housing options and living arrangements of low-income and no-income people.

In Chapter 1 we discussed how values are translated into legal norms and how legal systems may provide the formal premise for the establishment of the right to housing. We have also illustrated the limited impact of political declarations and enabling legislations. Indeed, if political and legal commitments were fully implemented homelessness would be reduced to a life style chosen freely among a multitude of existing housing and living options, probably by a small number of people. This being far from the reality under which people excluded from adequate housing make choices, homelessness and bad housing need to be situated in the context of structural features enabling and hindering access to housing.

Background factors which include demographic structure and population trends, the volume and features of the housing stock, and the magnitude of poverty in a population as a whole, operate through proximate factors of housing exclusion. Low level of household income, low access to affordable housing and low quality of low-cost housing may be identified as proximate determinants of housing exclusion. Only a small share of the population excluded from decent housing falls through family and public social safety-nets and becomes dependent on services for homeless people. The precariousness of low-income groups under conditions of chronic shortage of decent affordable housing provides fertile ground for extreme exclusion. Traumatic events such as domestic violence, breakdown of a relationship, loss of a casual job, chronic illness, may trigger off homelessness. The way people deal with the external constraints and traumatic events depends largely on their personality characteristics. On the one hand, people with particular personality characteristics may be less well equipped to struggle with hazards of social exclusion. On the other hand, particular personality characteristics may induce individuals to adopt behaviour which may exclude them from family solidarity and community care. Violent behaviour, alcohol dependence, drug abuse, may be directly associated to extreme social and housing exclusion.

It is the combination and the feedback between the complexity of background and proximate factors which induces housing exclusion and homelessness as its extreme manifestation. The phenomenon of homelessness cannot be reduced only to proximate determinants and even less to a single determinant.

Attempts to reduce the complex phenomenon of homelessness to one or two factors is generally a simple-minded attempt to put the blame for the condition on individuals. This becomes particularly evident when figures on alcoholism among the homeless population are used as explicatory factors of homelessness. The causal link needs to be meticulously examined for at least two reasons. As Koegel and Burman (1988) point out, there are many millions of well-sheltered alcoholics, and a substantial number of homeless people start drinking heavily after they lose a home. When background factors and proximate determinants of housing exclusion are not taken into account, and when the causal link is reduced to a single determinant, one may easily forget that:

> "Alcoholism knows no class boundaries, but homelessness clearly does" (Blasi, 1990; p. 210).

3.1. BACKGROUND FACTORS OF HOUSING EXCLUSION

The key structural features or background factors which operate as opportunity enhancing or abasing mechanisms, determining access by the underprivileged to housing in the European Union countries at the turn of the century are: household dynamics, housing supply and features of the housing stock, and access to financial resources.

We will focus our analysis on:
- the number and composition of households as the demographic background which gives an idea of the total housing needs of a population;
- features of the housing stock which indicate the type and the degree of (in)congruency between the housing supply and the demand;
- indicators of poverty which illustrate the magnitude of the population potentially exposed to housing exclusion.

3.1.1. Socio-demographic processes and expected changes in households

The most important socio-demographic changes observed during the past three decades or so, that have transformed family relations and household dynamics, comprise: declining number of children born to couples; decrease of nuptiality; increase in divorce rate; decrease in remarriage rate; increase of consensual unions; increase of one person households; increase of one parent families; changing home-leaving pattern of young adults.

The outcome of these processes are reflected in the decrease in the average household size and the increase in the number of households

Table 6: Structure of households and of dwellings

A - Distribution of households (%) by number of members, 1991

	1	2	3	4	5+	Average size
Belgium	28	30	19	15	8	2.5
Denmark	34	33	15	13	5	2.2
Germany						
FDR	34	31	17	13	5	2.3
GDR						2.4
Greece	18	28	20	23	11	3.1
Spain	18	23	21	23	22	3.3
France	27	30	17	16	10	2.6
Ireland	20	21	15	17	27	3.3
Italy	22	25	22	22	9	2.8
Luxembourg	22	29	22	16	11	2.8
Netherlands	29	31	15	17	8	2.4
Portugal	14	26	23	22	16	3.1
UK	25	34	17	16	8	2.5

B - Distribution of dwellings (%) by number of rooms, 1992

	1	2	3	4	5+	6+
Belgium	1	10	21	29	19	20
Denmark	6	18	23	26	14	13
Germany						
FDR	2	6	21	29	20	22
GDR						
Greece	--------14------		--------64------		----------22------	
Spain	0	3	11	26	36	24
France	6	13	24	28	18	11
Ireland	2	4	10	21	26	37
Italy	4	18	27	28	13	10
Luxembourg	2	3	10	20	20	45
Netherlands	--------10------		16	44	21	10
Portugal	---------6------		12	-------------82-----------------		
UK	---------7------		-------32------		---------61------	

Source: Commission of the European Communities, 1993a

as dwelling units (Tables 6 and 7). The salient features may be summarized as an increase in the variety of living arrangements when observed on the macro scale, and increased variation over a life cycle, with feminization and aging of households as outcomes of the interaction between demographic and socio-economic-cultural factors.

The complexity of processes that transform households implies that the particular features of life course patterns which result in emerging household structures, include both new phenomena with long term implications, and a variety of processes susceptible to short term fluctuations. Feminization and aging of households fall within phenomena of fundamental relevance with long term implications. The high frequency of female-headed households at younger ages is resulting from union dissolution and at high ages, moreover, is strengthened by gender differentials in longevity. On the other hand, the home-leaving patterns of young adults is far more susceptible to short-term changes in social policy. Changes in public allocation of resources may have a strong impact on the timing of transitions and reversibility of passages from one household form to another by young adults.

The above tendencies are being universally observed in the European Union countries, however, inter-country variations continue to exist. Within a country group variations, for instance among migrants or ethnic minorities, may also be witnessed. In less prosperous economies and among disadvantaged social groups, living conditions may prevent or delay the emergence of a greater variety of living arrangements which result from changes in individual expectations and terminal values. Indeed, in southern European countries and in Ireland the average household size is higher due to a higher share of households with five or more members and a lower share of one person households (Table 6 Panel A).

There is a wide consensus among demographers that the aging process is unavoidable and that in the forthcoming decades it will evolve relatively independently of fertility levels and the socio-economic development (Avramov, 1992; Cliquet, 1993). The demographic momentum in conjunction with changes in terminal values which have long-term effects will further affect structural transformation of families and households. There is a more or less general agreement that societies will have to accommodate the changing needs, especially of people living in aged households, one person units, and of lone parents.

While it may be expected that further diversification of household types will continue, the pace of change will depend on the mediating effect of living conditions. In recent times, changes in cultural standards are producing demographic effects and it is generally acknowledged that in the decades to come this might further extend and influence not only the demographic processes but more particularly family and household structures. Short term fluctuations in allocation of public resources may affect the timing but they are not expected to change the general tendency. Once individuals become acquainted with the welfare culture, personal standards and individual expectations continue to evolve.

There is clearly a high degree of congruency between structural characteristics of our societies and behavioural strategies of individuals. Modern societies are characterized by, and favour, rapid change, high differentiation and complexity, openness and mobility, multiple partial membership, broad middle stratum (Hoffmann-Nowotny, 1987). The existence of the welfare state is reflected in the culture and has its analogy in individual pursuit of desirable living arrangements.

Observed changes in households go clearly in the direction of major diversification and growth in the share of non-family households, namely one person households and consensual unions without children, and family households of a lone parent with unmarried children. We may expect a high frequency of female-headed single households in older age groups due to greater female longevity and high frequency of union dissolution. These changes imply increased need of social support for elderly households, especially of the very old, due to further extension of the life span and the fact that aging parents will have less, if any, (female) biological offspring to provide assistance and care. Furthermore, in the aging society not only basic existential needs will have to be accommodated but also the rising expectations of the elderly living alone.

3.1.2. Housing supply

While there is a general agreement about the direction in which household changes may be expected to evolve, there is little consensus about the impact of raising expectations and multiplication of opportunities for the well-off on the social condition of the very poor. Yet, the most visible, immediate consequence of changes in family and household patterns in recent decades is their impact on consumption, especially on the housing market. Indeed, while the rate of increase in the number of new dwelling units has manyfold exceeded the population growth, it has generally lagged behind household growth (Table 7).

Table 7:   Population, households, and housing stock increase, 1981-1991

	Population increase		Household increase		Housing stock increase	
	Number	%	Number	%	Number	%
Belgium	123,600	1.2	345,000	9.6	-62,700	-1.6
Denmark	22,400	0.4	221,000	10.6	213,100	9.6
Germany						
FDR	2,067,800	3.3	9,727,000	10.2	1,733,100	6.8
GDR	-711,900	-4.2	142,000	9.5	470,500	7.2
Greece	414,200	4.3	370,000	12.4	691,000	17.3
Spain	1,327,600	3.6	1,375,000	12.9	2,428,200	16.5
France	2,864,600	5.3	2,491,000	13.1	1,988,000	8.2
Ireland	86,000	2.5	118,000	13.0	134,100	15.0
Italy	1,266,900	2.2	1,825,480	9.8	1,295,000	5.9
Luxembourg	19,500	5.3	17,000	13.3	9,100	7.2
Netherlands	801,800	5.6	1,129,000	22.6	1,043,300	21.5
Portugal	39,600	0.4	252,000	8.6	729,500	21.2
UK	1,170,100	2.1	2,100,000	9.7	2,014,000	9.4
EU Total	9,522,200	2.8	20,112,480	17.0	12,686,200	9.5

Source: Council of Europe, 1992; Commission of the European Communities, 1993a

Only in Greece, Spain, Ireland and Portugal did the pace of increase in dwelling units exceed that of households. The high increase in the volume of the housing stock in Greece, Spain and Portugal is largely due to an enormous increase in demand for secondary residences. By way of example, the number of secondary residences almost tripled in Spain over a ten year period; the index of increase for 1981/1991 was 294 (Calculated from data: Commission of the European Communities, 1993a).

The structural discrepancy between available housing and the changing demand is reflected in a general housing shortage in some Member States. Although the total number of dwelling units in the European Union as a whole, exceeds the total number of households, there are marked variations between countries. The surplus of dwellings over households is marked in the Mediterranean European Union countries Greece, Spain, France, Italy and Portugal and is moderate in Denmark, Ireland and the United Kingdom.

By contrast, in four European Union countries the number of households exceeds the number of available dwellings. The shortage of dwellings of 5 per cent in Belgium, 4 per cent in West Germany, 7 per cent in Luxembourg and 3 per cent in the Netherlands may imply that a non-negligible number of households are doubling up. Indeed, figures show that there is a shortage of more than one million dwelling units in the four Member States (Table 8).

An important mediative factor which nuances the relationship between the offer and the potential demand, measured in terms of dwellings and households, is affordability of available dwellings. The elementary market law enters into effect when the demand is growing faster than the supply. Indeed, the past decade witnessed marked rent increases. The increased tension on the housing market due to the growing demand, keeps rents high which in turn makes access to adequate housing increasingly more difficult for the poor. The competition on the free housing market marginalized the poor in substandard and over-crowded dwellings, on the one hand, whilst at the same time, urban renewal marked a gradual disappearance of substandard housing which often implied the disappearance of cheap housing all together. For the poorest segment of the population the process may mark the passage from the condition of exclusion from adequate housing to homelessness.

In countries where the process of fragmentation of households which induced an unprecedented increase in the housing demand was initiated earlier, it may be expected that the number of households will continue to grow but at a somewhat slower pace from the mid-1990s onwards.

In southern European countries, peak growth, more particularly of one-person households, may be expected at the turn of the 21st century. Since a prevailing desire for space and detached housing may be

Table 8: **Population, households and dwellings in 1991**

	Population (in 1000)	Households (in 1000)	Dwellings (in 1000)
Belgium	9,987.0	3,953.0	3,748.0**
Denmark	5,145.4	2,251.0	2,139.0
Germany			
FRG	63,725.7	28,175.0*	27,139.0
DDR	16,027.6	6,652.0	7,033.0
Greece	10,112.7	3,344.0	4,690.0
Spain	38,993.8	12,040.0	17,154.3
France	56,893.2	21,535.0*	26,237.0*
Ireland	3,518.8	1,029.0	1,039.0
Italy	57,746.2	20,646.0*	23,232.0*
Luxembourg	384.4	145.0	134.7
Netherlands	15,010.4	6,135.0	5,965.0
Portugal	9,858.6	3,176.0	4,181.1
UK	57,511.0	22,800.0	23,750.0
TOTAL	344,914.0	131,881.0	146,678.2

* Data for 1990
** Occupied dwellings

Source: Council of Europe, 1992; Commission of the European Communities, 1993a

expected to persist (Louvot, 1992), tensions may be expected to be present in the housing market well into the next century. The housing situation of the underprivileged needs to be seen within the context of their position, their perspectives and their chances to compete in the housing market.

Not only is the growth in the housing stock inadequate but also the composition of the stock is changing much slower than the composition of households (Table 6 Panel B). If we look at the structure of the housing stock we observe a general shortage of small apartments. In countries with the highest share of one-person households, Belgium, Denmark, Germany, France and the Netherlands, on average, three out of 10 households consist of one person and only one out of 10 dwellings consist of one or two rooms. In general there is an overall shortage of two and three room apartments.

The trend towards smaller households may be expected to induce an increased demand for smaller dwellings (Louvot, 1992) but incomes will also play an important part in determining whether people will need to, and want to, change their housing situation following household changes over the life course of individuals and the family cycle.

In addition to meeting raising expectations of the better-off groups who show a desire for larger dwellings, individual houses and owning one's own home, the welfare societies are expected to meet the needs of the underprivileged. But, at the time of the major surge in housing demand, governments opted for decreasing social housing, deregulating the market and reducing the cheap housing supply. Indeed,

> "Since the end of the sixties there has been a trend away from large scale intervention by public authorities in the economic and social aspects of social housing, towards the present day type of intervention which restricts State involvement and subsidies and targets aid more precisely to the individual rather than to construction, alongside the deregulation of investment" (Commission of the European Communities, 1993b).

The problem, of course, lies in the fact that deregulation of investment resulted in rent increases on the formal housing market which are not compensated by the present level of direct transfer resources to low income households. Housing benefits and other provisions targeted at individual households are practically non-existent in a number of Members States, and are insufficient to provide access to decent housing for the most needy in the overwhelming majority of European Union countries.

Indeed, the housing authorities acknowledge that:

> "providing housing for people on low incomes will remain a problem" (Commission of the European Communities, 1993b).

The governments disengagement from the delivery of housing may prove to be in direct contradiction with the expectations of citizens of the state. In a 1991 Population Policy Acceptance Survey undertaken in nine countries of western, central and eastern Europe, a series of questions on welfare and solidarity addressed the issue of respondents expectations from the state. The welfare provisions from which the whole population benefits, namely health care and provision of adequate housing, were the domains for which governments are held completely or quite responsible by almost all the respondents (Avramov, 1995). In Italy 94 per cent of all respondents, in the Netherlands 83 per cent, and in Spain 95 per cent of respondents, held governments highly responsible for the provision of adequate housing for everyone. The perception of the degree of government's responsibility by the respondents cannot be entirely separated from their evaluation of the current level of public delivery and its efficacy. Indeed, it seems that the lower the level of public delivery is, the higher the citizen's expectations from the state are and the higher the consensus about the extent of government's responsibility in making adequate housing available for everyone is.

3.1.3. Poverty

Unemployment, more particularly long-term exclusion from paid labour, is a strong generator of social and housing exclusion. While unemployment affects all social categories (OECD, 1994) the same cannot be said for housing exclusion. However, long term unemployment exceeding four years, access only to casual and precarious low-paid jobs and low levels of social benefits insufficient to meet housing costs, result in a strong social and housing segmentation. The OCDE study on employment (1994) shows that four in 10 unemployed people have abandoned hopes of finding, and have stopped looking for employment, or have accepted a casual job. A large part of that population is dependent on minimum non-contributory benefits as their only source of income.

Poverty is not just lack of financial means but above all lack of opportunity to gain control over events in one's own life. In condemned and run down urban quarters generations born after mid-1970s are entering their teens and early adulthood without ever having seen their parents go to work regularly. The lack of opportunity in one's own family and social environment to perceive the advantages of education, qualification, paid work, and social cooperation, closes the circle of intergenerational transfer of poverty.

With respect to poverty and access to prosperity, two divergent tendencies may be observed in the Member States. On the one side, the number of people living below the poverty threshold has been decreasing, on the other, social segmentation has cut off the marginalized from access to prosperity. It is not only the fact that the gap between the well-off and the poor is increasing, but also that the very poor are excluded from basic human rights that characterises social inequities in prosperous economies at the turn of the century.

The relative prosperity, generally documented by data on the decreasing share of the population living below the poverty line (EUROSTAT, 1990; O'Higgins and Jenkins, 1990), and by changes in the consumption pattern of average households (EUROSTAT, 1992), needs to be qualified also from the perspective of the sub-groups which constitute the socially excluded minority. The latest published data show that some 53 million citizens of the European Union were poor in mid-1980. The share of those excluded from prosperity ranged from 5.9 per cent in Belgium, at the lower end of the scale, to 32.7 per cent in Portugal, at the upper end of the poverty scale. (EUROSTAT, 1990). It may be expected that more recent data, when published, will document a further decrease in the share of the population living below the poverty line in the early 1990s in more prosperous European countries. The average household consumption patterns as indicators of prosperity show that families in advanced welfare economies are spending a lesser share of their income on food and other basic necessities and are generally allocating more to leisure than in less developed European Union countries (EUROSTAT, 1992). A similar direction of change in consumption patterns may be observed within countries over the time span of the past two decades. Furthermore, it may be argued that the populations of the European Union countries are enjoying the historically unprecedented level of social rights which may be claimed through institutionalized channels of social solidarity.

The enlargement of the middle strata and the improvement of the living conditions of the population as a whole, was made possible by the general growth rate and by the redistribution policies. The social redistribution through social protection schemes, such as health and retirement from which the entire population benefits, and security schemes which enter into effect if loss of income occurs, have extensively contributed to the enlargement of the middle strata. These protection schemes have freed relevant parts of the family budget by relieving the financial burden on family members who would have been expected to provide directly for those in need at the time of need, had a generalized impersonal solidarity system not been set up.

128

A relative success in enlarging the middle strata and improving their living conditions during the past three decades or so, has masked the fact that those who were left out, or were dropped out of the channels which may give access to prosperity, are altogether left out of the prevailing system of social solidarity and may become disentitled to the basic human rights. Not only is the number of very poor people who depend on welfare benefits increasing but the social condition of the poorest seems also to be deteriorating. In Western Germany the number of beneficiaries of the minimum subsistence means had almost doubled between 1980 and 1988 as the percentage increase was 89 (Commission of the European Communities, 1993c). Furthermore, data on income distribution indicate that the historical tendency of the narrowing gap between the poorest and the richest has reversed direction in several countries. Notably in the United Kingdom in real terms,

> "between 1979 and 1990 the incomes of the poorest 10 per cent have fallen by 10 per cent while the incomes of the richest 10 per cent rose by 60 percent" (Bates, 1994).

The European Observatory on National Policies to Combat Social Exclusion in its Third Annual Report (1994) documented the tendency of the widening of the gap between the rich and the poor in several Members States. The most striking figures on the decrease of real earnings of the poorest segment of the population in the 1979-1991 period are for the United Kingdom. The Report highlights that the existing economic mechanisms are either an obstacle to the decrease of segmentation or are contributing to its increase.

Value added tax (VAT) rates do not seem to have a strong impact on redistribution of resources between the well-off and the poor. However, changes in the VAT introduced in Belgium in 1992 in order to meet European Union requirements document how the economic system may be modelled to benefit high and middle-income households to the detriment of low-income households.

> "The reform of VAT rates would on average bring in 12 ECU per household ... the most wealthy households would gain 105 ECU per year, whilst the poorest would pay out an additional 14 ECU" (Dumon and Nuelant, 1994).

3.2. INTERMEDIATE FACTORS OF HOUSING EXCLUSION

Background, macro factors of housing exclusion operate via mezzo structures which directly affect the concrete primary groups. Although consanguinal and conjugal families whose members do not co-reside create important sub-systems and solidarity networks, households are basic units defined by the actual living and housing arrangement. Households have been profoundly affected by changes in fertility, nuptiality and divorce during the past two-three decades and these changes are reflected in the structural transformation and multiplication of household forms.

Some household types, namely young single-person, and one-parent households, will be more exposed to the risk of income insufficiency and loss of a dwelling when their members have no access to a paid job. It is precisely those households which have increased substantially in number in recent decades and which are expected to continue to rise in the coming decades. Changes in the family dynamics are not affecting only structures of households but are also having an impact on the weakening of bonds and shrinking of the potential pool of relatives. The reason given by four out of 10 households for becoming homeless, among those accepted for housing as homeless by the English local authorities, is that parents, other relatives or friends are no longer willing or able to accommodate them (Department of Environment, 1993).

The impact of intermediate determinants of housing exclusion may be measured by the financial ability of different household types to access housing for rent. Access to publicly funded social housing and access to the free rental market may be considered as two basic variables of housing exclusion. The impact of structural factors of housing exclusion can be illustrated by the discrepancy between the offer and the demand of social housing, and by income insufficiency as an obstacle to access the commercial rental market. Our hypothesis is that households which are unable to earn a sufficient income on the free labour market to raise above the poverty line are unable to cover costs of adequate housing on the free housing market.

A ratio between the number of households with incomes below the poverty level and the number of social housing units for rent can be used as an indicator of the discrepancy between the offer and the

130

demand. The relationship between income insufficiency and access to the free rental marker may be illustrated by the share of income that low-earning households need to spend on rent in the commercial rental housing circuit.

Two categories of households, which depend on social security and which may need access to social housing in order to overcome the poverty trap, can be identified. The first group consists of households which are not currently generating any income or are earning insufficient income on the labour market (individuals may be retired, unemployed, unable to work,or otherwise needy) and which would be living in poverty if they were not benefiting from social security. The second includes households which live in poverty although they are benefitting from social security. The poverty threshold in any Member country is defined as 50 per cent of average disposable income per consumption unit (EUROSTAT, 1990).

Households with incomes below the poverty level before receiving social security may be identified as those potentially in need of social housing for rent. Households living in poverty and deprivation after receiving social security may be identified as those in acute need of access to publicly funded social housing for rent.

The ratio between the number of households which would be living in poverty if they were not receiving social security and the number of social housing units is used as a contextual indicator and not as a measure of actual housing demand. However, the ratio between the number of households living below poverty line after receiving social security, and the number of social housing units for rent in a country, may be considered more than just a general indicator. It is a measure of unmet needs. It indicates a threshold below which housing the poor cannot be addressed through formal recognition of rights or reforms of distribution policies.

If we compare the number of households which may be potentially in need of housing assistance with the number of social housing units for rent, it is evident that the current stock does not meet the potential needs of people dependent on social security in any of the Member Countries. The highest share of social housing for rent, 36 per cent, is found in the Netherlands. However, the share of households with incomes below the poverty level before social security in this country, like in most other Member States, is close to 40 per cent of all households (Table 9).

Data about the scale of social protection in the European Union countries show the importance of social transfers for the prevention of mass poverty and deprivation. Most important transfers are old-age and survivors pensions and sickness allowances, followed by a series of functions ranging from invalidity to housing. In the mid-1980s, in the European Union, the share of households with incomes below the poverty level before social security stood, on average, around 40 per cent of all households. After social transfers the share was reduced, on average, to 15 per cent of all households (Commission of the European Communities, 1993c).

Social security which encompassed a supply of social housing has, no doubt, played an important role in pulling a large segment of the dependent or low-earning population above the poverty level. The provision of social housing has in the past played an important role particularly in countries with the highest share of social housing for rent, namely, the Netherlands, Germany and the United Kingdom. However, even in these countries the level of supply has always been below the potential demand of people who are dependent on social transfers.

Data on poverty levels and the scale of social protection in Member States also show that the current system of transfers does not suffice to bring the income of all households above the poverty line (Commission of the European Communities, 1993c). Indeed, a significant proportion of the population remains poor and deprived. Households which remain poor even after receiving social security may be identified as those in acute need of access to publicly funded housing. In order to assess the extent of the discrepancy between the acute need and potential offer we will look at the number of social housing for rent and the number of households living in poverty (Table 9).

If in the European Union, as a whole, the population living below the poverty line was given statutory access to publicly funded housing, the current level of supply of social housing could be considered as sufficient, on average. However, there are marked differences between countries. The supply of social housing for rent in Greece, Spain, Luxembourg and Portugal is so low that it could not answer the needs of even a fraction of the poorest segment of the population. The current level of supply of social housing for rent could not meet the needs of the most needy in Italy and Ireland even if the available stock was assigned exclusively to households living in poverty. The supply would be just about sufficient in Belgium and France providing that households living below the poverty threshold were considered as the only needy households. The number of social housing units for rent exceeds the number of households living in poverty in Denmark, Germany, the Netherlands and the United Kingdom. The key issue in this group of countries is the level of demand for social housing for rent among the population eligible for social housing. In Denmark and the United Kingdom there is no income thresholds for the access to social housing, while in Germany and the Netherlands it is means-tested.

It should be clear that we consider the poverty level after social security transfers as an indicator of acute housing need, and not as a criteria for the allocation of social housing. When there is a large discrepancy between the offer and the demand, criteria for the allocation of meagre resources are not the key issue. When authorities engage in reforming the system of priorities for the allocation of resources which they deliberately keep at inadequate levels, reforms of criteria often result in the antagonization of undeserved groups which have to compete between themselves. Indeed, when a supply of social housing is insufficient, a priority given only to households who remain poor even after benefitting from social protection, would exclude households who just about manage to escape poverty by having access to publicly funded housing.

Due to the structural discrepancy between the magnitude of the population whose incomes are below the poverty level and the volume of the social housing stock for rent, reforming only the criteria for the allocation of social housing for rent would not suffice to meet the housing needs of low-income groups.

In the absence of a sufficient supply of publicly funded housing for rent, can an auto-regulated free housing market provide an answer to the housing needs of the poor? The policy makers seem to believe that it can. The social reality testifies to the contrary.

The impact of income insufficiency on housing exclusion can be illustrated by the share of income which needs to be spent for housing on the free rental market. We will use as indicators: the minimum subsistence means, as the lowest income level, and the price of rental

Table 9: Poverty and social housing: unmet needs

Country	Households below poverty level before social security, mid 1980s Number	Households below poverty level after social security, mid 1980s Number	Social housing for rent, early 1990s Number
Belgium	1,500,000	215,000	253,000
Denmark	n.a.	170,000*	429,000
Germany	13,800,000	4,200,000	7,755,000
Greece	1,200,000	650,000	0
Spain	n.a.	2,000,000*	208,000
France	9,500,000	3,100,000	3,775,000
Ireland	450,000	170,000	100,000
Italy	8,650,000	3,600,000	1,200,000
Luxembourg	52,000	10,000	2,500
Netherlands	2,200,000	400,000	2,176,000
Portugal	n.a.	970,000*	138,000
United Kingdom	8,850,000	2,500,000	5,806,000

Source: Estimated by the author on the basis of data from: Commission of the European Communities, 1993a; Commission of the European Communities 1993c; CECODHAS, 1995; * EUROSTAT, 1990

units in the cheapest urban district. The monthly amount of minimum subsistence means allocated to households consisting of a person living alone, couples with or without children and single parent families can be compared to average rents for dwellings of varying size.

We have chosen, by way of example, one of the least prosperous communes of the European capital, Brussels. The commune of St-Jans Molenbeek has the lowest average rent for all categories of rented dwellings, and the average rent is 24 per cent below the average for Brussels. The average rent in St-Jans Molenbeek amount to 277 ECU while the average for Brussels Capital is 365 ECU (IRIS, 1993;1). The total population of the commune of Molenbeek was 68,619 in 1993, the total number of rented dwellings stood at 16,748 in 1991 and accounted for 62 per cent of all dwellings. The maximum number of rooms for which rents are given in the report on the rental market is three, thus a more nuanced comparison between household size, minimum number of rooms to meet the needs of the household, and rent levels cannot be made for large households.

Table 10: Minimum subsistence means and average rents in St-Jans Molenbeek, Brussels in 1992

Household type	Guaranteed amount in ECU	Average rents in ECU according to the number of rooms		Percent of income
Person living alone	484	246	1 room	51
Couple with one child	740*	287	2 rooms	39
Couple with two children	877*	298	3 rooms	34
Couple with three children	1,056*	298	3 rooms	28
Single parent with one child	740*	287	3 rooms	39
Single parent with two children	866*	298	3 rooms	34

*   Monthly amount including family allowances. Since child allowances vary according to the age of the child, averages were calculated for ages 8, 10 and 12.

Source: Calculated by the author on the basis of data from MISSOC, 1993 and IRIS, 1993

However, even limited data provide a solid basis for the conclusion that rent levels are exceedingly high for low-income groups (Table 10). Data show that a person living alone on minimum subsistence means would need to spend 51 per cent of the income on rent, and a single parent with one child 39 per cent of the total income. When other housing costs, water, heating, gas, and electricity, are added, a lone parent would need to spend half of the total income solely on housing, and a single person would need to allocate at least 60 per cent of minimum subsistence means for housing costs. A couple with two or more children would need to spend some 40 per cent on rent and housing costs and still live under conditions of overcrowding.

The average rental market, even in the poorest communes and run down neighbourhoods, is inaccessible to people living on minimum incomes even when the housing component is directly or indirectly included in the benefit. In most countries the system of rent rebates applies only to social housing and not to privately rented dwellings.

Under conditions of a chronic shortage of cheap social housing, the only housing option for low-income groups has traditionally been within the substandard and marginal housing sector. But the decline in the number of social housing units for rent and the disappearance of condemned housing which traditionally secured low-cost, sub-standard housing for the poorest segment of the population is rapidly reducing housing options for the poor. Thus, all the proximate factors of housing exclusion; low household income, shortage of low cost housing, low quality of affordable housing and shrinking supply of substandard housing, are refracted through real income insufficiency as the key determinant of housing exclusion.

3.3. PROXIMATE DETERMINANTS OF HOMELESSNESS

The proximate determinants of homelessness are tightly interconnected and loss of a home occurs when a coincidence of a variety of situations occurs. It is precisely the accumulation of conditions, each of which on its own would not lead to a loss of a home, that pushes a person into homelessness. Lack of income and lack of qualifications are typically associated with the failure to gain control over events in one's own life. Income insufficiency is the predominant condition of housing exclusion, but it precipitates homelessness in conjunction with factors such as traumatic events and personality characteristics. Not every adolescent who has a family conflict clacks the door, and leaves a parental home, ends up homeless. But, a young adult without qualifications, without employment and without income, who experiences a breakdown of family solidarity will be in a particularly precarious situation. Ability to maintain and reconstruct social relations outside one's own family requires skill, knowledge, tolerance and time, assets which people in precarious conditions may not have.

A lack of income, and low income due to poor qualifications, a loss of access to income due to intrafamily violence or particular personality features, and finally a chance phenomenon, all have a cumulative effect on the trajectory into homelessness.

3.3.1. Income insufficiency

Unemployment and casual employment typically trace the path into shelters for homeless people. No income, low level of benefits claimed or low income earned on casual jobs, are unsurmountable obstacles to access to a personal dwelling for the overwhelming majority of people who turn to shelters for homeless people. In countries which implement minimum subsistence schemes particular conditions such as age, official domicile, minimum duration of residence in the locality, or eligibility for welfare only after all other rights have been vindicated, may exclude particular groups from access to benefits. The minimum age of eligibility for Revenu Minimum d'Insertion in France is 25, in Luxembourg 30, except for persons looking after a child or an invalid. Furthermore, minimum duration of residence for the foreign born population in this country is established at 10 years to gain access to the non contributory benefits in Luxembourg. In the United Kingdom single persons aged 18-24 are entitled only to 80 per cent of the entitlement for single, young adults above the age of 25. The right to the general non-contributory minimum is a residual right in Belgium and may be claimed only after all other rights have been exhausted, including for example an alimony.

When homelessness is directly associated to a traumatic event such as domestic violence, people faced with an abrupt loss of a home may face slow administrative procedures to claim financial assistance. Some may be unable to claim entitlements on their own and will need to be assisted.

At the time of entry into one of the shelters in Belgium four out of 10 homeless people had no income, two out of 10 were receiving unemployment benefits, one out of 10 was receiving minimum subsidence means. At the time when they leave a shelter, the number of homeless people without income is halved, and the number of those receiving minimum non-contributory benefits is doubled. This points in the direction of the conclusion that homeless people encounter administrative obstacles when claiming their right to minimum subsistence means and that they may therefore need assistance to do so. Reintegration into employment during the time of stay in shelters seems to be marginal.

At the time of entry 7 per cent of homeless people have an income from a paid job, at the time of exit 13 per cent earn an income.

In France, where minimum age for access to non-contributory benefits is 25, service providers for homeless people are registering a striking increase in demands for shelter by young people in the age group 18 to 25. Between the winter of 1993 and 1994 and autumn of 1994, the demand for shelter by young people having no income was estimated by more than half of surveyed service providers to have increased (FNARS, 1994). Among 100,000 homeless people sheltered by Le Secours Catholique in 1993, 35 per cent had no resources whatsoever or would have had no money left had they paid rent for a room (de Gouy, 1994). Half of the sheltered homeless people were unemployed and were looking for employment.

In Luxembourg four out of 10 homeless people entering a shelter were unemployed and looking for a job, two out of ten had a low-paid job.

3.3.2. Traumatic events

Family conflicts undoubtedly trigger off homelessness. When young adults with no qualifications and no employment experience a conflict in the family of origin, and when they are not eligible for social assistance due to their age or simply because social services are not there for them to turn to, shelters for homeless people are the only alternative to sleeping rough or squatting.

There is a general consensus among service providers that young adults cannot be properly assisted in available shelters and urgent accommodation. In France one in five homeless adults may be a victim of shortage of temporary accommodation within existing services. The lack of adequate institutional framework to assist people who suffered a traumatic event at one point in their life course and who become homeless, opens the door to a sequence of traumas. The National Federation of Associations providing Shelter and Social Rehabilitation (FNARS) stresses the dangers to which young people living in the street are exposed. The world of drug addicts, alcoholism, prostitution and violence becomes a daily reality. In the United Kingdom and Ireland homeless youngsters may be sheltered by the local authorities in bed and breakfast accommodation and left to wonder the streets during the day.

Family break down, and more particularly conjugal violence to which women are exposed, is increasingly pushing women into homelessness. Four out of 10 demands for urgent shelter in France were motivated by family breakdown. Four out of 10 sheltered women in Scotland reported having been forced into homelessness by domestic violence.

Deinstitutionalization of mental care and release of patients from hospitals marks a traumatic passage into homelessness for people who are still in need of care, but do not obtain care from their families or the local community.

3.3.3. Personality characteristics

The cognitive and emotional features of personality structure play an important role in the way people shape their life course and deal with living circumstances. The level of intelligence, emotional stability, border cases of mental health problems, and mental diseases, play a role in the chain of determinants of homelessness. Mental disabilities due to low intelligence or specific forms of psychopathology may require the type of care that families, more particularly low-income and low-skill ones, are unable and unwilling to provide. Emotional instability may be conducive to drug abuse, alcoholism, and other health problems which exclude individuals from family networks.

The modern approach to optimal mental care of patients suffering from psychopathologies which do not require hospitalization, presupposes that families and community provisions will be there to assist people unable to live a fully autonomous life. However, deinstitutionalization of mental health care has not been associated with adequate social provision of alternative care. The modernization of psychiatric treatment which was not accompanied by alternative therapeutical communities, has propelled people in need of care into homelessness throughout the European Union.

The situation reported in the Netherlands summarizes the complexity of the interaction between an individual's psychiatric problems, institutional care and financial cuts made by authorities, in aggravating the problems of homelessness. Efforts to contain costs of health care produce particularly ambiguous and often dramatic effects in the domain of psychiatric care. At the time of the rising pressure on psychiatric units, financial cuts are making it increasingly more difficult for people to become eligible for treatment.

> "The waiting lists are growing and so is the waiting time. In order to minimize the costs per patient and to maximize the numbers of treated persons, the period of admission is kept as short as possible. Furthermore, there is a strong tendency that psychiatric hospitals only treat persons for whom it is clear that treatment will be successful. Treatment possibilities are therefore becoming an important criterion for admission. This means that a homeless person with his/her often multiple problem is often being regarded as not treatable" (de Feijter and Radstaak, 1994; p. 12)

Those homeless people with low cognitive ability, those on the border line of clinical mental disease, and people with substance abuse, require assistance and care from the therapeutical community which is often not there for them.

3.4. HOMELESSNESS AS A SOCIAL PROBLEM

Why does homelessness cause such public concern today? Figures seem to provide an obvious answer. On an average day as many as 1.1 million people may be dependent on public and voluntary services for shelter and priority housing. Over the course of a year at least 1.8 million people in the European Union cannot afford the comfort of a home. Organizations working with the homeless have documented that the number of people who turned to public and voluntary organizations for assistance because they could not afford a decent dwelling has been increasing throughout the 1980s and early 1990s. On the basis of data on pressures on services for homeless people and estimates about homeless people who are paying for their temporary accommodation in the commercial circuit of furnished rooms or who are casually doubling up with friends and relatives, the extent of homelessness over the course of one year can be estimated at between 2.3 and 2.7 million people. If the tendencies observed during the past decade persist in the 12 Member States, the number of homeless people who may be expected to depend on public and voluntary services could reach 6.6 million by the turn of the century.

Furthermore, homeless people are not the only people experiencing housing exclusion. In the early 1990s as many as 15 million people are living under severe housing stress in substandard and overcrowded dwellings.

However, numbers and growth rates do not provide a sufficient explanation for the senzibilization of the general public over the plight of people excluded from adequate housing. The number of homeless people does not explain the mobilizing effect of their call for action. Concerns over the increase in homelessness and its life-long impact on people who at some point in their life are living in the street, sleeping in an emergency shelter, or in temporary accommodation, need to be perceived in a broader historical and social context of the images of poverty. Concerns over the social implications of homelessness on the society as a whole, need to be seen in the context of solidarity and interdependence of individuals and social groups in the increasingly more complex societies.

In the broader historical context it may be argued that the level of homelessness and bad housing in the second half of the 20th century in more prosperous European economies, is the lowest ever observed in human history. Indeed, historically, the security of a decent dwelling has been the privilege of the minority. Until the early 20th century the majority of the population of Europe lived in precarious dwellings without sanitary facilities, under conditions of overcrowding and personal insecurity of tenure. Today, the vast majority of European Union citizens live in well equipped, spacious, personal dwellings. The prevalence of well housed and decently housed people provides a historically new context for the perception and analysis of homelessness. The manifest forms of poverty, homelessness and bad housing, which were a constant in human history have become unacceptable today. Indeed, pressures are increasing to translate the terminal values such as prosperity and solidarity into practice, not only for the majority but for all citizens regardless of their individual characteristics or markers of group identity.

In this section we will illustrate how changes in values are affecting the perception of poverty, solidarity and responsibility. We will look at the evolution of normative standards pertaining to the conceptualization of solidarity and the transfer of resources to the socially vulnerable groups.

3.4.1. Impact of value systems on the perception of homelessness

The genesis of the ideal that an individual is a value *per se* may be traced through philosophical and religious postulates and a multitude of social theories (Dumon, 1986; Avramov, 1993). Its universalistic roots may be found in the Judeo-Christian tradition, which emanates the vision of individuals being equal before God, in the constitutions of modern states which proclaim equality of citizens before law, in the 20th century social legislations aimed at opportunity enhancing. The concept of intrinsic worth of all human beings has become the cornerstone of international human rights law by enshrining the right to "inherent dignity of human person" in the Universal Declaration of Human Rights (1948).

The ethical premises of the valorization of the individual may not be considered as the invention of modern times, but rather as a constitutive element of western philosophy. However, only the contemporary societies have codified individual rights as universalistic principles. The individual, regardless of his/her adherence to a religious, political, or social group, and irrespective of his/her gender and concrete merits and contribution to the society, is at the centre of the value system.

The ideology of valorization of the individual, implicitly recognized for centuries, is evolving into a coherent system of ideals, values and institutions only in modern societies. Only developed societies can provide institutional guarantees which enable the pursuit of individual needs in a multitude of personalized ways. In the past, an individual's life course was heavily conditioned by demographic events. Disease and death were constants in life, affecting all age groups. In the traditional demographic regime, one quarter of infants died in the first year of life, one half of children died before reaching the age of 20. An adult who reached the age of 50 would have experienced deaths of 9 close family members, two to three would have been his own children (Fourastie, 1959). High mortality and high fertility were such proximate determinants of living conditions that little space was left for free choice and pursuit of individual life styles. Changes in the demographic regime, namely mortality control in the 19th century and fertility control in the 20th century, were indispensable conditions for valorizing the individual. However, they were not a sufficient condition. Only the conjunction between demography and the evolution of the welfare society could open the path to the multiplication of individual options. It is the flexibility of the advanced system of institutionalized solidarity which guarantees dignified living conditions, personal development, education, health care, and social protection on a non-discretionary basis, which can provide the conditions for the valorization of individuals.

With the growing prosperity of the second half of the 20th century, standards of personal happiness, quality of life and expectations towards oneself, one's children and the society changed rapidly. Shifts in cultural patterns, observed through the content of intergenerational transfer of values and norms, have been extensively documented in the general value surveys, such as the Eurobarometers and the European Value Systems Study. The European Value Study, as a major international research project has been analysing the nature of changes in moral, social and religious values, attitudes and beliefs in contemporary society.

The most striking features of observed value changes over the past twenty years, have been the decreased importance attached to the accumulation of personal wealth and greater striving towards a better quality of life. The perception of the controversy between having and being (Fromm, 1976) by the generations whose formative years coincided with the technological advances and economic growth without precedent, contributed to the major valorization of inherent human potential. Higher standards of quality and increased expectations are affecting both the perception of the immediate human condition and the quality of the social and physical environment.

Empirical evidence from value studies documented the multiplication of ethical systems and the dispersion of authority. Together with the increased variation in values, attitudes and beliefs, researchers have observed the diminishing prevalence of concerns for purely material prosperity. The emphasis on self-expression and quality of life is being expressed by the growing number of post-materialists (Inglehart, 1977; 1990). The motivational basis of the shift towards less materialistic values may be explained within the theoretical framework of the hierarchy of human needs and the degree of relative satisfaction (Maslow, 1970). Needs conducive to development are seen as indivisible components of motivation. Deprivation of lower basic needs may entail non-emergence of higher order needs, such as the need for realization of individual potential. This implies that full individual development is possible only under optimal living conditions.

Changes in values seem to be affecting all age groups but were most marked among generations that entered adulthood in the 1970s and 1980s (Lesthaeghe and Moors, 1990). The culture shift is influencing all domains of human activity, work, politics, religion, family, sexual behaviour, and social solidarity.

> "The incentives that motivate people to work, the issues that give rise to political conflict, people's religious beliefs, their attitudes concerning divorce, abortion, and homosexuality, the importance they attach to having children and raising families - all these have been changing. One could go so far as to say that throughout advanced industrial society, what people want out of life is changing." (Inglehart, 1990 p.3)

The value studies have documented how changes in cultural paradigms have been associated with the formative experience of generations socialized under conditions of fast technological advances, economic growth and increased educational attainment. These background processes have created favourable conditions under which young adults could set higher personal and social goals and which could lead to higher levels of tolerance towards social ambiguities.

A drift away from having towards being and aiming at the higher quality of life is not affecting in the same way all population sub-groups, all age groups or all countries. Inglehart finds that post-materialistic values are more widespread among cohorts born after 1945. A high degree of correlation is found between the overall level of development and the percentage of people who shared post-materialistic values. Indeed, the highest share of post-materialists was found in the Netherlands, the lowest in Portugal. Finally, some social groups may be inclined to express militant opposition to modernity and to manifest intolerance towards diversity as a reaction against radical changes which are taking place faster than the social group can internalize them.

The multiplication of value systems and higher levels of tolerance have been associated with changes in complex systems of beliefs and postulates developed by social groups in order to pursue external adaptation and internal integration (Barnes, 1990). These systems are integrated into the content of the intergenerational transfer of culture and cannot be taken as mere behavioural changes and passing fashions. Due to the strong dynamic interaction between culture and structure, changes in the macro system are associated with changes in values, which in turn influence choices affecting social structures.

The increased value attached to personal autonomy and valorization of the individual is reflected through the growing pressure on the political authorities and on the social institutions to implement opportunity-enhancing instruments.

> "No longer need we rest on sheer viability and survival as our only ultimate proof that poverty or war or domination or cruelty are bad, rather than good. We can consider them bad because they also degrade the quality of life, of personality, of consciousness, of wisdom." (Maslow, 1970, p. 104)

Images of poverty and homelessness are today strongly associated with perception of poverty as the lack of adequate opportunities and homelessness as the loss of all opportunities. The concept of exclusion generally used to name homeless people as those excluded from decent housing, and poor as those who are socially excluded, implies rejection and prevention from access and participation. It puts emphasis on the external obstacles and mechanisms of rejection rather than on the individual characteristics of victims of exclusion. The culpabilization of the victims of exclusion has by no means disappeared, but it is being questioned by a growing number of people, victims of exclusion and advocates of their rights, social researchers, activists, citizens. In the societies which are evolving towards a knowledge-value model, the cognitive mobilization among the general public is acquiring dimensions which make it difficult for the policy makers to ignore the impact of social rights movements.

Public concern for 1.8 million homeless people who turn to public and voluntary services for shelter, in a population of 345 million of the European Union, needs to be seen as part of the culture shift occurring in one of the most prosperous sub-regions in the world. The political pragmatists may be tempted to affirm that the number of homeless people in developed countries may be considered as statistically marginal. However, the number of people who perceive the mere existence of homelessness as an unacceptable manifestation of the extreme lack of opportunity, may by no means be taken as marginal. Exclusion from housing is increasingly seen as a blatant breach of the social contract founded on the recognition of the right of individuals to the inherent dignity of a human being, and the commitment of political and social institutions to ensuring the valorization of individuals and dignified living conditions, to the maximum of a country's available resources.

A comprehensive evaluation of the current anti-poverty policies by the general public has not received sufficient and systematic research attention. The available data, however, confirm that Europeans attach high value to social protection and that they expect governments to improve and not to disassemble the system. In a 1992 Eurobarometer survey, respondents were asked whether they would favour social security benefits for everyone even if it implied increasing taxes. Seven out of 10 said "yes" (Commission of the European Communities, 1993c). In a recent Eurobarometer study, eight out of 10 respondents in the 12 European Union countries answered that the poor are insufficiently protected (Ferrera, 1993). Seven out of 10 European's think that the public authorities are not doing enough at present to fight against poverty and social exclusion (European Commission, 1994).

Indirectly, some tentative conclusion may be drawn from the policy acceptance surveys in the domain of family life and welfare (Moors and Palomba, 1995). The European Union countries which participated in the survey were Belgium, Germany, Spain, Italy, and the Netherlands. The survey results document that the expectations of citizens towards institutionalized solidarity on a non-discretionary basis are very high (Avramov, 1995). On average, in the countries in which housing was addressed in the questionnaire, eight out of 10 respondents answered that governments are completely or quite responsible for the specific task of making adequate housing available to everyone. The willingness to share the costs of policy measures is largely dependent on the policy aims. The findings for Belgium concerning the degree of solidarity with families point in the direction of the conclusion that citizens are prepared to express far higher degrees of solidarity than they are expected to under current policy schemes (Avramov, Callens and Cliquet, 1995).

But, while values and opinions may provide a framework for the interpretation of changes in the perception of and (un)acceptability of poverty and homelessness, they do not suffice to provide a full understanding of determinants of solidarity and the societal pressures to translate general principles into coherent social and legal systems. Changes in

146

values that have affected the culture shift towards paradigms valorizing the individual, referred to as post-materialism (Inglehart, 1977), post-industrialism (Bell, 1976) or post-modernism (Sakaiya, 1991), may be said to be reinforcing, rather than determining, the fundamental basis of human cooperation and solidarity.

3.4.2. From the principle of solidarity to the obligation of solidarity

Solidarity may be defined as the social expression of the community of interests, objectives and responsibilities. The need for human cooperation is generally explained by the vulnerability of the individual, precariousness of the human condition, the need to reinforce group cohesion, and the need to control unnecessary violence. The rational for social solidarity is generally based on the premise that the mutual interdependence of members of a society offers the basis for the social organization founded upon the complementary interests of individuals and of social groups. In the mind of most people, social solidarity is based on a set of ethical principles without much reference to the functional basis of altruistic behaviour. The utility of altruism is usually described in moral terms.

But, why would people comply with the social expectation that they behave so as to achieve positive outcomes for another rather than for oneself? While individuals may perceive their interest in cooperating and sharing with kin and friends, and reciprocating to people with whom they interact, it is less obvious why they may be expected to behave altruistically towards the homeless people who may be perfect strangers and who may never be in a position to reciprocate.

Indeed, in the advanced societies which developed impersonal institutionalized channels of solidarity and transfers of resources, two questions are frequently raised: on whom is solidarity imposed, and who benefits from it? The answers to such questions are imminently controversial because in large anonymous societies, benefits cannot be calculated in terms of individual gains. Furthermore, because of the way questions are asked, the answers can be based only on proximate indicators of personal wealth, rather than on background determinants of individual and social welfare.

The fundamental theoretical explanation of the determinants of human cooperation has come from the field of evolutionary theory, rather than from social sciences. The seemingly obvious premise that natural selection should favour competition, cheating and nepotism, faced socio-biologists with the challenge of explaining the genetic survival value of innumerable examples of cooperation and altruistic behaviour. The cumulative effect of research carried out by social biologists and evolutionary theoreticians resulted in the development of theory documented by the empirical evidence of the human struggle to increase inclusive fitness, promote reciprocal altruism and enhance cooperation.

The evolutionary theory explains the nature of altruistic interaction between kin as the striving to increase inclusive fitness (Hamilton, 1964). This implies that the net positive benefit to the individual for promoting the welfare of another at one's own expense, is based on the drive to ensure that one's own genes are transmitted to the next generation. Altruism between non-kin in face-to-face situations generally operates within a system of perceived payoff, but the net positive benefit and survival value of altruistic behaviour towards strangers may seem less obvious. Nevertheless, the analyses based on the game theory and the experimental situation known as the Prisoner's Dilemma has demonstrated, in a quantitative way, the long term advantages of reciprocal exchange motivated by altruism (Axelrod, 1984; Casti and Karlqvist, 1995). Game simulations demonstrate that selfish behaviour may be advantageous only in the short term, while the value of cooperation in repetitive situations, with an unlimited number of interactions, exceeds, by far, the benefits of selfishness. Cooperative behaviour on a repetitive basis is ultimately more profitable for both parties than selfish behaviour. The payoff of cooperation when two altruists interact is higher even from the point of view of self-interest, than when self-interested individuals interact and strive to achieve only their own individual payoff. Axelrod (1984) summarized the nature of benefits:

> "TIT FOR TAT won the tournaments not by beating the other player but by eliciting behaviour from the other player that allowed both to do well...so in a non-zero sum world, you do not have to be better than the other player to do well for yourself. This is especially true when you are interacting with many different players... The other's success is virtually a pre-requisite for doing well yourself" (Quoted from Casti and Karlqvist, 1995 p. 74 and 75).

Models of reciprocal altruistic behaviour have also shown how selection can operate against the cheater (Trivers, 1971) and the extent to which societies can increase the amount of altruistic behaviour (Rushton, 1980; Nowak and Sigmund, 1993). The societal implications of the functional advantages of exchange motivated by altruism are paramount. Indeed, societies which developed more effective social forms of cooperation proved to be more successful (Cliquet, 1994).

The ultimate explanation of the genetics of altruism is that altruism is self-serving behaviour. Provided there is no cheating, it results in the net fitness increase to all parties. However, the innate behavioral predisposition to behave altruistically operates together with other predispositions, such as the predisposition for competition and nepotism. The evolutionary theory shows that the human being in his genetic endowment is a typical example of evolutionary compromise between cooperation and competitive drives. In his social relations man is permanently confronted with frustration: he wants to compete but he has to cooperate to enhance his development (Cliquet, 1994). The long-term increase in socio-cultural viability and development is imminently tied to the social reinforcement of altruism. Indeed, pressures to induce sharing behaviour operate through channels of collective consciousness, of duty and of legal obligations. These mechanisms of social pressure are necessary to diminish the payoff of selfishness and to introduce sanctions for non-cooperation.

Since cooperative behaviour is perceived as an important component of social success, and as altruism can be reinforced by learning and sanctions against defectors, the most important domains of human activity no longer rely on individual motivation and willingness to cooperate, but rather on institutionalized channels of social solidarity. In large, anonymous nation-states the first examples of institutionalized altruism were associated with national defense and the control of epidemics, whereas the more recent examples are associated with universal education and entitlement to minimum subsistence means.

Thus, the basis for solidarity and transfers of resources may not be perceived only in terms of individual values and ethical systems. Solidarity entails much stronger social pressure to comply with accepted principles than any set of values. Indeed, the social obligation to behave altruistically and express solidarity is the pressure to comply with the behavioral patterns which are increasing the viability of social structures and promoting socio-cultural evolution.

Of course, human behaviour cannot be explained only in terms of evolutionary biology. Psychological, cultural and philosophical components of human motivation and behaviour may not be underestimated. However, what genetics of altruism tell us about the nature and functional basis of altruistic behaviour, makes a narrow sighted, often evoked, perception of altruists as those on the giving side and beneficiaries as those on the receiving side, unsustainable. It documents that altruistic behaviour provides an important payoff to altruists and that social interaction between altruists provides greatest payoff for all participants. Thus, promoting altruism may be considered as the enlightened long-term self-interest of society.

The socio-cultural payoff of cooperative strategies may be identified through evolving systems of social protection based on transfers of resources and services between individuals, social groups and generations upon which contemporary socio-cultural and economic viability builds. Complex social structures and terms of social cooperation require a degree of permanency of protection guarantees. Social solidarity cannot be used as a traffic sign which may be pointed towards one or the other destination, or be replaced at convenience. The premise of institutional solidarity is that it is accessible to all members of a society who are in need, irrespective of their merits or capability to reciprocate.

3.4.3. Needs, merits and minimal entitlements

It is generally acknowledged that the well established system of pooling of public resources and their redistribution between social groups has largely contributed to the overall efficacy and development of advanced technologies in the 20th century. Until recently, the redistribution system was based on the premise that direct flows of resources should be made between those who are, or have been, contributing to their creation in the labour market. People who were not in paid labour had entitlements either as dependent family members or were excluded from social solidarity and could rely only on charity. A further step in social development marks the divorce of individual market-based merits from minimal social entitlements.

Identification of universal human needs and social commitment to their enhancement, form the binding social texture of contemporary societies. By contrast, rejection of socially vulnerable people from channels of social solidarity, may have a long-term eroding effect. It increases awareness of risks and of the provisional nature of social security schemes. Indeed, homelessness, as the manifest form of extreme exclusion, is a phenomenon eroding the social fabric by increasing the sense of individual isolation and system inadequacy. It reinforces the feeling of insecurity among the population as a whole in the face of multiple life-long risks, from unemployment and precarious financial conditions to hazards of disease and old age.

It may be said that the fulfilment of all human needs is socially regulated and controlled, but collective provision of minimal entitlements is restricted to only a very few of the basic ones. An assortment of basic human needs according to a relative hierarchy and the nature of needs, on the one hand, and the balance between policy choices and available resources, on the other, form the basis for social negotiations of terms of assistance and control. Basic needs, such as the need for food or health care, may be pursued in a multitude of personalized ways, but minimum institutional provisions are established in all European Union countries for people who are not able to provide for themselves or to care for themselves. The basic human need for shelter is generally recognized but the minimum provision of decent housing for all remains to be implemented even in the most prosperous economies.

Once the basic human needs are acknowledged as universal rights, their provision transcendents an evaluation of individual's merits and their capacity to reciprocate. Indeed, merits of a sick man are no longer examined prior to the provision of medical assistance. But, even when the basic need for shelter is recognized as a universal right, the desperate appearance of a homeless person, once poverty and lack of community care have taken their toll, may be a frequent reason for non-assistance.

Why does the toll of poverty and dependence so often provoke contempt? Are homeless people free-riders benefitting from the social redistribution of resources without contributing to the social wealth? Are they responsible for their own misfortune? Are homeless people victims?

The perception of responsibility generally nuances degrees of individual and social solidarity. It operates twofold, through distinction between personal responsibility for one's own condition and events beyond the person's control, and through identification of "relevant others" who are held responsible for providing assistance. Dependency which is perceived as a consequence of events that are beyond the individual's control is generally viewed more sympathetically (Rushton, 1980) and *vice versa*. Indeed, responsibility is a key element determining the degree of political, juridical and financial commitment to solidarity. Unwillingness to transfer resources to homeless people is generally associated with attempts to put the blame for the condition on the victims, and to transfer the responsibility for homelessness on the excluded themselves.

The analysis of background factors of housing exclusion undoubtedly points to the conclusion that there are structural obstacles to access to housing and decent living conditions in the overwhelming majority of European Union states. In the United Kingdom, homelessness legislation distinguishes the meritorious and un-meritorious homeless and the intentionally and non-intentionally homeless. By accepting in 1993 to house 159,974 households as homeless, the authorities indirectly acknowledged that several hundred thousand people may become homeless through no fault of their own.

Under conditions of structurally induced exclusion from adequate housing and exclusion from any housing, the principle of entitlements becomes the cornerstone for breaking down the ideology of culpability of the disadvantaged and the undeserved. The acknowledgement of rights is the first step in the recognition of social responsibility and a step away from arbitrary assistance and charity towards collective responsibility and institutional provision. Removing obstacles to access the right to housing and the provision of means to maintain the right is the next step. But, both in terms of the formal recognition of rights and the actual provision of means the European Union countries are still in mismatch.

Chapter 4

CONCLUSIONS
AND POLICY IMPLICATIONS

This report confirms the persistence of homelessness in the European Union at a serious level, with all the attendant human suffering that this entails. This final chapter gives an evaluation of the legislative approaches as a response to homelessness, and sums up the conclusions of the study.

4.1. RIGHT TO ADEQUATE HOUSING

The right to adequate housing can be fully, legally established and adequately implemented only when defined as an individual entitlement that can be claimed. In order to implement the right it does not, however, suffice to identify the individual as a titular, but it is also necessary to clearly identify the public authorities responsible for removing the obstacles to access to the right. Under conditions of structurally induced housing exclusion, an equitable access to the right necessitates, furthermore, a clear identification of the undeserved segments of the population as target groups for the positive discrimination. Homeless and badly housed people, unable to compete on the formal housing market, can effectively gain access to the right to housing only under terms of preferential treatment.

The establishment of the right to housing, as a legally enforceable claim secured to a person by law, entails a complex political and juridical process. It requires a firm policy commitment of governments to enhance the right to housing, it implies the establishment of the right in national legislation, the provision of means to enable equitable access to the right, the monitoring of the implementation of juridical and social policy dispositions, and may need the continuous affirmation and reaffirmation of principles by the social partners and citizens in order to promote and to maintain the acquired rights.

4.1.1. Recognition of international principles

As a statement of intent, the commitment to promote the right to adequate housing has been made by all Member States through instruments of international law. The commitment to the community of nations was made directly by the governments of Belgium, Denmark, France, Germany, Greece, Ireland, Italy, Luxembourg, Portugal, Spain, the Netherlands, and the United Kingdom. All Member States have adopted principles codified in the Universal Declaration of Human Rights and have ratified the International Covenant on Economic, Social and Cultural Rights which directly recognizes the right to adequate housing. Although international law does not have the legal instruments to specify concrete rights and duties evolving from the formal recognition of the right to housing, the United Nations documents may be considered as important standard-setting instruments. However, most states which have ratified these documents appear to treat them as aspirational and have given little, if any, attention to their operationalization. It is extraordinary that governments should sign international agreements yet shaw so little concern for their legal and ethical implications.

The European intergovernmental organizations have not incorporated the right to adequate housing as a legal principle in the regional conventions, charters and treaties. The right to housing is not explicitly recognized as a universal principle nor as an individual entitlement in the European Convention on Human Rights and in the European Social Charter. Since the Council of Europe does not explicitly recognize the right to housing in the European Convention on Human Rights, individual claims to a home cannot be made before the Court of Human Rights, as they may be made for political and civil rights enshrined in the Convention. The European Social Charter does not include a policy

154

commitment to the right to housing, neither does it put any obligation on states to provide adequate housing to all its citizens.

The European Union does not address the right to housing as a legal principle and reserves no competence over housing issues. Under a particular interpretation of the principle of subsidiarity, Member States have exclusive competence to deal with housing issues.

The fact that the right to housing has not been incorporated in the key European conventions, charters and treaties, may be explained by a higher degree of commitment which the European standard-setting instrument entails. If the right to housing as a social right acquired the same "weight" as the commitment to some political and civil rights it would entail a clear obligation for a state to provide housing for its undeserved citizens. The monitoring of implementation by the international community would then operate as a legitimate instrument of external control over the (non) compliance of governments with the commitment to establish the right to adequate housing.

It would, however, be unrealistic to expect governments to ratify a document which would include a commitment to implementation at a European level, prior to achieving a national consensus about the need to establish the right to adequate housing. The analysis of the legal framework pursued in Chapter 1 shows that there is little consensus among Member States on the feasibility of incorporating the commitment to the right to housing made to the community of nations in the domestic legislation.

4.1.2. Forms of recognition of a right to housing

Up to now, only four Member States, Belgium, Portugal, Spain and the Netherlands have enshrined the right to housing clause in the constitution as the highest law of the land. The right to housing in these countries is integrated in the programme part of the constitution and is established as a statement of intent or commitment to principles, rather than as an entitlement. Individual legal claims to a home cannot be made exclusively upon constitutional provisions.

The recognition of the right to housing as an individual entitlement which is needed if governments are to make a step further than just a statement of intent, entails operationalization of principles through legal provisions and social policy measures. France and Belgium have passed laws to transform the right to housing into concrete legal norms. The laws in the two countries assert, clearly and in a detailed manner, the right to housing for all citizens and the obligation of solidarity towards those unable to access the right from their own resources. In the United Kingdom and Ireland, laws have been passed which do not assert the general right to housing but specifically address the condition of homelessness. The legislation in the United Kingdom puts an obligation on the local authorities to provide housing for those homeless people assessed to be in priority need. Irish legislation puts a duty on the local authorities to monitor homelessness and assess the housing needs of people excluded from adequate housing.

However, the right to housing, as a right derived from the right to dignified living conditions, recognized by all Member States, is directly or indirectly incorporated into the legislative system. The most important legal bases are established in anti-poverty and housing legislation. The loss of income which may occur due to unemployment is dealt with in all Member States and unemployment benefits are established in their legislation. However, welfare benefits, as non-contributive entitlements for people able and willing to work but who have never had access to paid labour and for those whose unemployment rights have been exhausted, are guaranteed in the basic national legislations of only eight countries: Belgium, Denmark, Germany, France, Ireland, Luxembourg, the Netherlands and the United Kingdom. The general minimum income schemes are established in the legislation of some autonomous communes in Spain and some regions and provinces of Italy. Greece and Portugal have no general minimum subsistence entitlements. Housing supplements to the non-contributory benefit may be provided in Germany, France, Ireland, Luxembourg, the Netherlands, the United Kingdom, and in some regions of Italy.

The right to housing, as established in the housing legislation of Member States, may imply that homeless people are given statutory priority in the allocation of publicly funded housing, that their condition may be taken into account, or that it may even exclude them from access to publicly funded or state-subsidised housing. Access to social housing by homeless people and people at risk of becoming homeless may be said to be, in principle, an enforceable claim only in France and the United Kingdom. In Belgium, Denmark, Germany, Ireland, Luxembourg and the Netherlands, a number of permissive legal provisions and policy measures enable preferential allocation of publicly funded housing to the homeless people. In the four southern Member States, Greece, Portugal, Spain and, to a lesser degree, Italy, permissive legal provisions, even when put in place, are not effectively accompanied by policy measures. The result is that homeless people have low-priority access to subsidized housing and may be weak competitors under the prevailing distribution system.

The rent control system has largely been eroded in all Member States and the main policy orientation builds on a model of market-conformist social housing with market rents. The social character of the housing policy is expected to be maintained through individual rent rebates and direct transfers to target households.

4.1.3. Operationalizing the right to housing

Although shortcomings can be identified in the formal legal system which is largely permissive rather than mandatory in most Member States, the major stumbling point in the process of establishment of the right to housing lies outside the normative framework. The provision of means to enable the enforcement of the legislation is the main obstacle to access to housing by the homeless. In the four southern European Union countries, Greece, Spain, Italy and Portugal, shortcomings in the establishment of the right to housing are still rooted in the legal framework which does not guarantee minimum subsistence means and does not establish equitable access to the publicly funded housing for no-income and low-income groups. In the remaining eight countries, Belgium, Germany, Denmark, France, Ireland, Luxembourg, the Netherlands and the United Kingdom, it may be said that the legal premise for the establishment of the right to housing exists, albeit to a different extent. Our analysis shows that obstacles to access to rights defined within the existing legal framework occur because:

- the law is not applied;
- inadequate resources are earmarked;
- certain groups are deliberately excluded from entitlements;
- income thresholds for access to publicly funded housing are too high;

- multiplication of administrative and juridical procedures is not accompanied by the clear identification of duties;
- social housing favours housing segregation.

In addition to the lack of a clear and explicit recognition of the right to housing as an individual entitlement, the lack of enforceability of the existing legislation, the lack of clear identification of responsibilities and duties of governments and administrations, the lack of comprehensive identification of target groups, the inconsistent monitoring of implementation, the uncritical evaluation of the efficacy of used legal instruments and policy measures, and the insufficient allocation of resources, form a chain of obstacles in the process of the establishment of the right to housing as an individual entitlement.

4.1.4. Lack of convergence

The ways in which Member States address the right to housing and housing exclusion in their national legislation show no signs of convergence. There is no evidence that Member States have consulted with each other to share models of policy and practice in their legislative approaches to homelessness. Considering the scale of the homeless problem, this is difficult to understand. The only clear convergence, which directly affects homeless and badly housed people, may be identified in the policy orientation of all Member States to disengage from the provision of publicly funded and state-subsidized low-cost housing. The policy option is reflected in the legal system which addresses housing as an asset rather than as an individual entitlement. The implication is that no-income and low-income people who cannot acquire an asset on the free housing market may be disentitled from at least one human right, the right to an adequate home.

The policy choice to rely on the market mechanisms to meet the housing needs of the population is, however, accompanied in all Member States by some social correctives. These correctives can be established in the country's legislation and explicitly address the right to housing or the condition of homelessness, but they may also operate extensively, or even exclusively, within the framework of generous social policy. This may be the reason why it is not possible to determine a causal link between the formal recognition of the right to housing and the extent of housing exclusion. If one was to give an example of the Member

State with the most effective preventive and responsive policy to deal with housing exclusion it would, no doubt, be Denmark. This is a country where the right to housing as an individual entitlement is not enshrined in the domestic legislation and where local authorities do not have a statutory obligation to provide housing to homeless people. It may be said that in Denmark access to housing is an accomplishment of the comprehensive social policy and measures, rather than of the legislative system.

4.1.5. The advantages of a housing rights approach

Where there is a high level of legal commitment to general welfare provisions and where there is a high degree of political consensus on the need to provide adequate housing to homeless and badly housed people under the welfare framework, there may seem to be no additional benefits of the codification of the right to housing as an individual entitlement. This is the approach taken in Denmark, the Member State with the most advance system of housing protection, and in the Netherlands. However, Belgium, another country with a generous welfare system, has recently codified the right to housing in the domestic legislation. In the forthcoming years it may become possible to compare trends and features of homelessness in countries with similar welfare provisions but with different degrees of legislative commitment to the right to housing.

However, there may be measurable and important advantages of the codification of the right to housing in domestic legislation. Such advantages are, broadly speaking, as follows. Laws guarantee a higher degree of permanency because they may be less easily revoked than social policy measures. Thus, it may be said that the translation of principles underlying the social policy and welfare provisions into statutory legal norms may be an insurance policy for the future. As long as social policy measures effectively provide access to housing, the incorporation of the right to housing may not seem relevant. However, the establishment of the right to housing as a legal principle, is a guarantee that solidarity will be maintained even when there is not such a high degree of consensus among the political elites on the need to provide for the undeserved.

In socially more heterogeneous states, the legal grounds may be the only feasible way to ensure equitable access to housing and the permanence of social protection for the undeserved segments of the population. Under conditions of the conflicting aspirations of different political groups, advantages of social protection based on principles of solidarity need to be institutionalized through the legal system in order both to maintain the rights acquired, and to implement those which have been promised.

Laws are important instruments of standard-setting. They set public attitudes and have a bearing on the manner in which public officials, administrators and policy makers approach particular categories of citizens. Laws encourage the accountability of governments to citizens and public bodies. They are, ultimately, the explicit statement of society's values, concerns and the level and nature of its sentiments of social solidarity. All these are compelling reasons for believing that legislative approaches to homelessness have considerable merit. From this study it is apparent that legal and legislative responses to homelessness have been applied either insufficiently, ineffectively or so unevenly as to produce meagre results. In those countries and regions where either a right to housing has been laid down and operationalized, or where indirect rights to housing derive from the social security code, homeless people have benefitted and responses to homelessness have been more systematic and effective. Those are compelling reasons for both an improved national legislative framework and a more sophisticated, systematic and effective international legal approach to having rights for homeless people. The laying down of such an improved, effective and honoured system of housing rights for homeless people is a challenge which now confronts the international community, Member States and advocates for homeless people.

Advantages of the non-discretionary nature of legal rights which guarantee objectivity of treatment may be recognized as one of the important sets of prerequisites for access to the right to housing by the undeserved segment of the population. The existing laws, however, do not suffice to remove the structural obstacles to access to adequate housing for everyone. The present level of commitment of governments to the process of realization of the right to adequate housing is generally limited to the recognition of the right as a moral quality which constitutes an ideal to be achieved in the future, rather than a legally enforceable claim secured to a person by law.

4.2. PEOPLE EXCLUDED FROM ADEQUATE HOUSING

The discrepancy between the normative and the actual is reflected in the incidence of homelessness and bad housing, conditions which affect people unable to compete for adequate housing on the formal housing market. The right to housing, as defined in major standard-setting documents and domestic legislation, addresses the right to adequate housing and not just the right to shelter. Consequently, not only the people sleeping rough or in shelters for homeless people or squatting, but also badly housed people, constitute the population whose rights are breached because they cannot access adequate housing.

The homeless and those living under severe housing stress share the common reality of people who, due to their income insufficiency and lack of affordable housing, are experiencing social marginalization and may be exposed to progressive exclusion from the most important domains of human activity. Both homelessness and bad housing are factors of life and health threatening environmental hazards. Exposure to environmental hazards due to the lack of a home or overcrowding, disrepair, no access to sanitary facilities, environmental degradation, is associated with ill health, disability, psychological stress, developmental constraints, lower life expectancy, housing and social segregation, and may be associated with obstacles to accessing social deliveries of services such as education, adequate health care, and culture.

4.2.1. Homeless people

In the minds of most people homelessness is associated to the condition of tramps and vagrants. At best, homeless people will be identified with people with no fixed abode. But, the homeless population extends far beyond the most visible condition of those sleeping rough and squatting or those classified administratively as people lacking abode. They are in fact the smallest, even though the most visible part of the homeless population. People in temporary shelters provided by the public and voluntary services and those in rented rooms on short term basis who have no security of shelter and no prospects to access a personal dwelling are the most numerous part of the nucleus of homelessness. People assisted by the public and voluntary sector because they have no home and on their own could not afford any accommodation are those who have exhausted their private coping strategies and are dependent on social solidarity. Those paying for their precarious accommodation in rented rooms often in sub-standard housing or bed and breakfast are those who are able to pay for their own temporary shelter but have no access to a home.

Homeless people are compelled to be the most spatially mobile of the excluded. Being allowed to stay in sheltered accommodation only for a limited duration and being able to afford and find casual accommodation on a short-term basis, they will pendulate between different forms of housing exclusion. Typically, individuals will move frequently from one accommodation arrangement to another. Thus, there may be no clear cut line separating people who have no accommodation and are in temporary accommodation in dormitories, boarding houses or hotels provided as urgent shelter by the public or voluntary organizations, from those people in precarious dwellings at the margin of the regular rental market. People without a dwelling may move between situations which near anything from sleeping rough, squatting, staying in urgent accommodation provided by public and voluntary organizations which may be shelters for homeless people or hostels, guest houses, asylums and hospital annexes.

Homelessness as the outcome of the social process of impoverishment which results in exclusion of the poor from adequate housing, and homelessness as the outcome of exclusion from community care which results in the inability of people in need of care to maintain a personal dwelling, affect people who have little control over their own life. In the world of advance technology and high social mobility, the degree of control over events in one's own life ultimately determines the position of the individual in the society and the quality of his/her life. Chance events play an important role in individual's life, they may, indeed, enhance or reduce life options. However, individuals deal with external constraints according to their ability to be flexible and socially mobile. In this social context, mobility and flexibility are imminently founded on the potential access to a multitude of options from which individual choices may be made. In the social reality of the European Union countries, which are among the richest in the world both in terms of income and individual life style options, homeless people are those who are least equipped to deal with external constraints and who have little control over events in their own life. The spacial mobility of homeless people and their pendulating between different forms of housing exclusion may be perceived in terms of chance determined by external constraints, and not choice.

4.2.2. The extent of homelessness

On the basis of available sources, we have estimated that on an average day at least 1.1 million people in the 12 Member States are dependent on public and voluntary services for homeless people. Over the course of the year as many as 1.8 million people may find themselves homeless and in extreme housing need. These figures may give a realistic image of the extent of homelessness among people who have exhausted their private coping strategies and are dependent on public resources. However, they do not include people in boarding houses and furnished rooms who are paying for their own temporary accommodation or are casually doubling up with friends and relatives, partly because they can still rely on private networks, partly because there are no public services to turn to. Indeed, organizations working with the homeless indicate that on the basis of the demand for shelter and housing, the minimum estimates of the extent of homelessness in the European Union should be increased, on average by 30 to 50 per cent. This would imply that in the 12 Members States of the European Union between 2.3 million and 2.7 million people may be in need of shelter and urgent housing over the course of the year.

From the European Union perspective, it may be said that countries with high standards of general welfare protection, namely Belgium, Denmark, Luxembourg and the Netherlands, have implemented more efficient policies and measures to deal with the prevention of homelessness. France, Ireland, Germany, and the United Kingdom have been less successful in removing structural obstacles to access to adequate housing. These countries have devised a number of programmes to deal with consequences of exclusion, namely by making services for homeless people available. It should be clear that available services are neither sufficient in number to meet the needs, nor efficient in terms of reintegration of homeless people into housing and into social activity. However, a relevant number of public and voluntary services operate, and a high number of homeless and potentially homeless people turn to them when they are available. In the group of southern European Member states, a low number of people known to have been homeless, tells us more about lower standards of public delivery of social protection and provision of shelters for homeless people, than they do about the extent of housing exclusion.

The magnitude of homelessness in different member States reflects not only different degrees of efficacy of the social protection and housing provision, but, also the general socio-cultural background against which individuals in difficulty develop their coping strategies to deal with housing exclusion. People who cannot compete on the formal housing market generally resort to three basic strategies. They may turn to the public and voluntary services if they are available, they may have to rely on relatives and friends if they are willing and able to provide, and they may resort to "unconventional dwellings" when they cannot turn to the public services or kin and friends because they are not there for them.

Indeed, a high number of homeless people who turn to public and voluntary services in Germany, France and the United Kingdom, when compared to the extend of homelessness in large southern European countries such as Italy and Spain, need to be perceived within the context of public services available to people excluded from adequate housing. Under the prevailing system of structural obstacles to access to adequate housing in these countries, the more public services are made available to homeless people, the more homelessness becomes visible. The magnitude of homelessness in Germany, France and the United Kingdom, reflects both structural obstacles to access to adequate housing and the extent of public services made available to people who cannot compete on the housing market. Under conditions of similar structural obstacles in the southern Member States, considerably lower standards of public and voluntary assistance to people who cannot access adequate housing are reflected in relatively low numbers of people who can turn to service providers. People have no other choice than to resort to their private coping strategies.

Indeed, the extent of "unconventional" housing in southern countries is generally much higher than in other Member States. Tens of thousands of people living in shacks, tents, caravans, containers, staircases, elevator cages and other "unconventional dwellings" complement the picture of extreme housing exclusion in countries where very few public and voluntary services are available to homeless people and where authorities make no statutory commitments to assisting people in housing need. Finally, under conditions of lower standards of public delivery of services in the group of southern Member States, family networking is stronger. Kin solidarity remains an important buffer against extreme social and housing exclusion, more particularly amongst young adults and families in the early phases of the family building process.

A cross-country comparison of the extent of homelessness and housing stress is, no doubt, necessary both for research and policy purposes. Our aim was not to count the number of excluded people for statistical purposes. Our aim was to evaluate the impact of current social and housing policies on housing exclusion in the European Union, and to asses the level of unmet housing needs at the European level. In order to address housing needs in each Member country, the extent of homelessness needs to be qualified within a national context. Whether the number of homeless people will be perceived as very high, high, moderate or low, will depend on the point of reference. Indeed, in countries with generous welfare policies, a seemingly low number of homeless people, when seen from a transnational perspective, may be evaluated as unacceptably high within a national perspective. More particularly in terms of unnecessary human suffering in prosperous economies.

For the overwhelming majority of people who experience homelessness it is not a life-long condition. But the fact that, for the majority of people who loose a home homelessness may be a transitory state, does not make it less important. The impact of homelessness needs to be perceived not only in terms of duration but also of the time in individual's life cycle when it occurs. Homelessness is experienced increasingly at the delicate moment of the passage into adulthood. It is precisely at the time when young adults need to establish personal relations, access economic activity and enter early stages of the family building processes, that homelessness marks their life prospects. Homelessness experienced by young families, which is also on the rise, marks in a traumatic way the life of several generations.

4.2.3. The extent of severe housing stress

Exclusion from a personal dwelling marks the condition of homelessness. Exclusion from adequate housing in terms of quality and security defines the condition of badly housed people as those living in insanitary, sub-standard, overcrowded, insecure dwellings. On the basis of data on severe overcrowding and sub-standard accommodation, we have estimated that severe housing stress affects at least 15 million people in the European Union countries. Twice as many, or 30 million people, may not be able to enjoy the comfort of a shower or a bathroom in their dwelling.

Our analysis shows that close to 18 million European Union citizens are homeless or extremely badly housed and living under severe housing stress. They may be considered as the nucleus of the population whose right to adequate housing is breached.

4.3. DETERMINANTS OF HOUSING EXCLUSION

Homelessness and housing exclusion occur against background factors which operate as opportunity enhancing or abasing mechanisms determining access by the underprivileged to housing. Background factors include demographic structure and population trends, the volume and features of the housing stock, and the magnitude of poverty in a population as a whole, and they operate through proximate factors of housing exclusion. Low levels of household income, limited access to affordable housing and low quality of low-cost housing may be identified as key proximate determinants of housing exclusion.

Only a small share of the population excluded from adequate housing falls through the family and public social safety-nets and becomes dependent on services for homeless people. However, the precariousness of low-income groups under conditions of chronic shortage of decent, affordable housing provides fertile ground for extreme exclusion when other external constrains occur. Traumatic event such as domestic violence, breakdown of a relationship, loss of a casual job, or chronic illness, may trigger off homelessness. The way people deal with the external constraints and traumatic events depends largely on their personality characteristics. On the one hand, people with particular characteristics may be less well equipped to struggle with hazards of social exclusion. On the other hand, particular personality characteristics may induce individuals to adopt behaviour which may exclude them from family solidarity and community care. Violent behaviour, alcohol dependence, or drug abuse, may be directly associated with extreme social and housing exclusion.

It is the combination and the feedback between the complexity of background and proximate factors which induces housing exclusion and homelessness as its extreme manifestation. The phenomenon of homelessness cannot be reduced only to proximate determinants and even less to a single determinant.

4.3.1. The key structural obstacles to the access to housing

Insufficient supply of affordable housing may, however, be identified as one of the key factors of housing exclusion in the European Union countries. The policy choice to abandon the option of providing low-cost social housing in favour of market-conform housing is reflected in the general decline in supply of low-cost housing and in the increase of rents for newly built housing funded or co-funded by public resources. While general tendencies take the same direction, that of lesser supply of public housing, differences in the share of social housing in the total housing stock still reflect past policies on the provision of social housing. However, the general demand for social housing and access to publicly funded housing by homeless people is dependant on numerous factors and cannot be determined by the simple illustration of the share of social housing units in the overall housing stock.

Three factors play a key role in determining housing options of the poor: the level of supply of social housing, the distribution policies underlying access to publicly funded housing and the system of rent rebates.

Our analysis shows that the current level of supply of publicly funded housing for rent does not meet the potential needs of households dependent on social protection in any Member country. The number of households which do not earn an income to raise above the poverty threshold and which are pooled out of poverty by the system of social protection exceeds the number of social housing units for rent in the European Union.

The provision of social housing for rent in six out of 12 Member States, could not meet the needs of households living in poverty even if they were considered as the only households in need of housing. The number of households which remain below the poverty threshold even after benefitting from social protection exceeds the number of social housing for rent in Greece, Spain, Ireland, Italy, Luxembourg and Portugal. The most striking discrepancy between the potential need and the level of delivery can be illustrated by figures for Spain. In Spain 2,000,000 households living below the poverty level may be competing for 200,000 units of social housing for rent. In Greece, Italy, Portugal and Spain, access to social housing is still largely a work related benefit and homeless people who are generally excluded from regular paid labour, may be also excluded from publicly funded housing.

The distribution policies, rather than the actual supply, may be said to be a more valuable indicator of access to publicly funded housing for homeless and badly housed people in Member States in which social housing for rent exceeds the number of households living in poverty. Indeed, policies underlying the distribution of the stock of social housing are quite different in the Member States. The system of allocation of social housing and the degree to which homeless people can have access to publicly funded housing does not show signs of convergence at a European level. People living below the poverty line do not have statutory access to publicly funded housing in any Member Country. In France and the United Kingdom, homeless people have in principle statutory access to social housing. In Belgium, Denmark, Germany, Luxembourg and the Netherlands, homeless people may have preferential access to publicly funded housing. In Belgium and France, the number of social housing units for rent is at the critical level when it could be estimated as sufficient only if households living below the poverty line were considered as the only households needing access to social housing for rent.

The anti-poverty measures as an answer to unemployment, and more particularly to long-term unemployment, are of particular relevance for the prevention of extreme housing exclusion. However, they can be efficient only in combination with the sufficient supply of public housing and preferential access to social housing by the homeless. Our analysis shows that deregularization of investment into housing resulted in rent increases on the formal housing market. High rents cannot be compensated by the current level of direct transfers to low-income households. The average rental market, even in the poorest communes and run down neighbourhoods, is inaccessible to people living on minimum incomes. A person living on minimum subsistence means may need to spend 60 per cent of his income on rent and basic housing services. A couple with two or more children would need to spend some 40 per cent of their minimum subsistence means on rent and housing costs and still live under conditions of overcrowding.

4.3.2. Housing the poor

The way governments deal with the structural obstacles to access to adequate housing for everyone, and the means they made available to people to deal with the external constraints show no signs of convergence. The only real consensus between the governments of the Member States is at the level of the prognosis that under free market conditions housing the poor will be a problem.

Indeed, unless social correctives in the form of comprehensive preventive and responsive policies are introduced, housing exclusion may continue to affect millions of people even in prosperous economies. Preventive policy measures need to ensure assistance through risk situations over the life course of individuals and life circle of families. The responsive measures need to be aimed at social and housing reintegration of people once housing exclusion has reached homelessness as its final stage. They may need to include personalized services which go beyond the provision of housing and include social healing and care for people who experienced marginalization and traumatic events. Responsive measures entail a high degree of urgency but cannot be considered as a substitute for social protection which prevents people from becoming destitute in the first place. A sufficient provision of publicly funded housing for rent, a comprehensive system of rent rebates and housing benefits and efficient therapeutical community services are the key provisions needed to enable the poor and people in need of care to access and maintain an adequate personal dwelling. The implementation of preventive policies entails a long-term perspective, a comprehensive social protection system and in many Member States may require fundamental social renegotiation of terms of institutional solidarity.

Research shows that Europeans attach high value to social protection based on principles of solidarity. Indeed, in a broad context of contemporary culture and social structures, public concern for 1.8 million homeless people who turn to public and voluntary services for shelter, in a population of 345 million of the European Union, needs to be seen as part of the culture shift occurring in one of the most prosperous sub-regions in the world. The political pragmatists may be tempted to affirm that the number of homeless people in developed countries may be considered as statistically marginal. However, the number of people who perceive the mere existence of homelessness as an unacceptable manifestation of the extreme lack of opportunity, may by no means be taken as marginal.

Images of poverty and homelessness are today strongly associated with the perception of poverty as the lack of adequate opportunities and homelessness as the loss of all opportunities. Exclusion from housing is increasingly seen as a blatant breach of the social contract founded on the recognition of the right of individuals to the inherent dignity of a human being, and the commitment of political and social institutions to ensuring the valorization of individuals and dignified living conditions, to the maximum of a country's available resources.

When politicians exhaust all their ideas as to how to generate development and promote the well-being of citizens, they tend to reiterate the opinion that individuals know best how to address their own needs and promote their own interests. While the statement may hold true for people who are well equipped to deal with the external constrains, it undermines the well established fact that a society is more than just a mechanical sum of competing individuals and that solidarity is the binding texture of a society.

REFERENCES

ALDRIDGE, R. (1994)
Homelessness in Scotland. In: CARLISLE, D., **1994 National Report on Homelessness, United Kingdom**. FEANTSA, Brussels

ALDRIDGE, R. (1993)
Homelessness in Scotland. FEANTSA, Brussels

ASSOCIATION DES MAISONS D'ACCUEIL (1993)
Amascopie. Association des Maisons d'Accueil, Bruxelles

ASHCROFT, S. (1993)
Report on Homelessness in England and Wales. FEANTSA, Brussels

ATD QUART MONDE (1994)
Rapport général sur la pauvreté, réalisé à la demande du Ministre de l'Intégration Sociale. Fondation Roi Baudouin, Bruxelles

AVRAMOV, D. (1995)
Welfare and Solidarity. Results from the Population Policy Acceptance Survey about the Respondents' Expectations from the State. International Colloquium Proceedings Attitudes on Population in Europe, Population and Family Study Centre, 24 March, Brussels

AVRAMOV, D., M. CALLENS, R. CLIQUET (1995)
Belgium: A Family Friendly Climate as the Valorization of Individuality. In: MOORS H., R. PALOMBA (Eds.), **Population, Family and Welfare, A Comparative Survey of European Attitudes**, Volume 1, p. 81-102. Clarendon Press, Oxford

AVRAMOV, D. (1994)
Short Term Projections of the Demand for Shelter in the European Union. Manuscript

AVRAMOV, D. (1993)
Porodica i stanovnistvo u raskoraku. Naucna Knjiga, Beograd

AVRAMOV, D. (1992)
Changing Structures of Families and Households: An Overview. In: UNITED NATIONS, **Changing Population Age Structures, 1990-2015, Demographic and Economic Consequences and Implications**. United Nations, Geneva

AXELROD, R. (1984)
The Evolution of Cooperation. Basic Books, New York

BANE, M.J., D.T. ELLWOOD (1986)
Slipping into and out of Poverty: The Dynamics of Spells. **Journal of Human Resources**, 21 (1)

BARNES, S. (1986)
Politics and Culture. Monograph Series, Institute for Social Research, Ann Arbor

BATES, P.J. (1994)
Housing and Homelessness. Report of the National Conference, Swanwick, 26-28 April

BELL, D. (1976)
The Culture Contradictions of Capitalism. Heinemann, London

BELERGEY, M.J.M. (1995)
Rapport général. **Actes du séminaire Exclusion, égalité devant la loi et non-discrimination**, Les éditions du Conseil de l'Europe, Strasbourg

BLANC, C.S. et al. (1994)
Urban Children in Distress. UNICEF, Gordon and Breach Science Publishers

BLASI, G.L. (1990)
Social Policy and Social Science Research on Homelessness. **Journal of Social Issues**, 46, 4, 207-219

BOOTH, A., J. EDWARDS (1976)
Crowding and Family Relations. **American Sociological Review**, 41

BRANDT, P. (1992)
Estimates on Homelessness in Denmark, personal communication to the Danish National Institute of Social Research, Copenhagen

BUTLER, K. (1994)
Homelessness in the 1990s: Local Authority Practice. Shelter, London

C.N.I.S. (1994)
Premières propositions pour un système statistique sur les sans abri et les personnes exclues du logement. Groupe de travail du C.N.I.S. sur les "sans abri", Paris

CARITAS -IRS (1994)
La casa: il rischio e l'esclusione. Rapporto sul disagio abitativo in Italia a cura di Tosi A., Franco Angeli, Milano

CARLISLE, B. (1994)
1994 National Report on Homelessness, United Kingdom. FEANTSA, Brussels

CASTI, J.L., A. KALQVIST (1995)
Cooperation and Conflict in General Evolutionary Processes. John Wiley & Sons Inc., New York

CECODHAS (1993)
A Roof over the Head of Every European: 5 Years of Involvement and Action. Brussels

CECODHAS (1995)
Le logrement social dans l'Europe des 15. L'Observatoire Européen du Logement Social, No. 13

CENTRE FOR HUMAN RIGHTS (1993)
The Human Right to Adequate Housing. Fact Sheet No. 21, United Nations Office, Geneva

CHASSÉRIAUD, C. (1993)
La grande exclusion sociale. Rapport au Ministre des Affaires Sociales, de la Santé et de la Ville. République Française, Ministère des Affaires Sociales, de la Santé et de la Ville, Direction de l'Action Sociale

CLIQUET, R. (1993)
The Future of Europe's Population. Population Studies No. 26, Council of Europe Press, Strasbourg

CLIQUET, R. (1994)
Inleiding tot de bio-antropologie. Universiteit Gent, Faculteit van de Politieke en Sociale Wetenschappen, Gent

COHRE (1994)
Legal Provisions on Housing Rights, International and National Approaches. Utrecht, The Netherlands

COMMISSION OF THE EUROPEAN COMMUNITIES (1994)
European Social Policy, A Way Forward for the Union. A White Paper, Office for Official Publications of the European Communities, Luxembourg

COMMISSION OF THE EUROPEAN COMMUNITIES (1993)
European Social Policy, Options for the Future. Green Paper, Office for Official Publications of the European Communities, Luxembourg

COMMISSION OF THE EUROPEAN COMMUNITIES (1993A)
Statistiques sur le Logement dans la Communauté Européenne. DG V, Brussels

COMMISSION OF THE EUROPEAN COMMUNITIES (1993B)
Funding of the Social Housing. 5th Meeting of the European Ministers of Housing, DG V, Brussels

COMMISSION OF THE EUROPEAN COMMUNITIES (1993C)
Social Protection in Europe. Office for Official Publications of the European Communities, Luxembourg

COMMISSION OF THE EUROPEAN COMMUNITIES (1992)
Social Europe, Towards a Europe of Solidarity: Housing. Supplement 3/92, Brussels

COMMISSIONE D'INDAGINE SULLA POVERTA E L'EMARGINAZIONE (1992)
Secondo rapporto sulla povertà in Italia. Franco Angeli, Milano

COMMITTEE OF MINISTERS (1993)
Recommendation No. R.(93)1 to Member States, Council of Europe, Strasbourg

COMMUNAUTÉS EUROPÉENNES (1993)
Union européenne - Recueil des traités. Tome I, Volume I. Office des publications officieelles des Communautés européennes, Luxembourg

CORIJN, M. (1993)
Leefvormen in Vlaanderen. CBGS Monografie 1993/2, Centrum voor Bevolkings-en Gezinsstudiën, Ministerie van de Vlaamse Gemeenschap, Brussel

COUNCIL OF EUROPE (1992; 1994)
Recent Demographic Development in Europe. Council of Europe Press, Strasbourg

COUNCIL OF EUROPE (1993)
Resolution 244 on the Right to Housing and its Implementation by Local and Regional Authorities. Standing Conference of Local and Regional Authorities of Europe, 28th Session, 16-18 March 1993

COUNCIL OF EUROPE (1993)
Homelessness. Council of Europe Press, Strasbourg

COUNCIL OF EUROPE (1961 and 1965)
The European Social Charter. Council of Europe Press, Strasbourg

COUNCIL OF EUROPE (1950 and 1953)
The European Convention on Human Rights. Council of Europe
Press, Strasbourg

CRISIS (1994)
Shelter/Crisis Winterwatch report 1993/94. Shelter, London

DALY, M. (1994)
Right to Housing Right to a Future. FEANTSA, Brussels

DANISH NATIONAL INSTITUTE OF SOCIAL RESEARCH (1994)
Duration of Stay of Sheltered Homeless People in Denmark.
Statistical Documentation, Copenhagen

DANMARK STATISTIK (1993)
Statistiske efterretninger 1993:4, **Social sikring og retsvaesen.**
Kobenhavn

DE GOUY, A. (1994)
**Sans-abri en France. Rapport Français pour l'Observatoire Euro-
péen des Sans-Abri**. FEANTSA, Bruxelles

DE FEIJTER, H., H. RADSTAAK (1994)
Homelessness in the Netherlands, Trends and Developments.
FEANTSA, Brussels

DEHAES, V. (1994)
**Leven van de bijstand. Een onderzoek naar de persistentie van
de armoede in Vlaanderen**, CBGS Monografie 1994/1, Centrum
voor Bevolkings- en Gezinsstudiën, Ministerie van de Vlaamse
Gemeenschap, Brussel

DELEECK, H., L. DE LATHOUWER, R., VAN DAM, K., VAN
DEN BOSCH (1990)
**Social Indicators of Social Security, A Comparative Analysis of
7 Countries.** Centre for Social Policy, Antwerp

DEPARTMENT OF ENVIRONMENT (1993)
The English House Condition Survey. HMSO, London

DEPARTMENT OF ENVIRONMENT (1991)
Homelessness Code of Guidance for Local Authorities. HMSO, London

DEPARTMENT OF ENVIRONMENT (1993)
Housing Statistics Bulletin. Republic of Ireland

DEVLIN, E. (1994)
HLM - Low Rent Housing: The French Social Housing System. International Conference Housing the Poor in Europe, Bradford 15-16 September 1994

DRAKE, M. (1994)
Homeless People in Europe and Their Rights. FEANTSA, Brussels

DUMON, W., T. NUELANT (1994)
European Observatory on National Policies, Trends and Developments in 1992. Commission of the European Communities, DGV, Brussels

DUMON, L. (1986)
Essays on Individualism, Modern Ideology in Anthropological Perspective. The University of Chicago Press, Chicago and London

EPSTEIN, Y.M. (1981)
Crowding Stress and Human Behaviour. **Journal of Social Issues**, 37, 1

EUROBAROMETER (1994)
The perception of poverty and social exclusion in Europe 1994. DGV, Brussels

EUROPEAN OBSERVATORY ON NATIONAL POLICIES TO COMBAT SOCIAL EXCLUSION (1994)
Third Annual Report, Robbins D. et al. Commission of the European Communities, DG V, Brussels

EUROSTAT (1992)
Europe in Figures. Office for Official Publications of the European Communities, Luxembourg

EUROSTAT (1991)
Population and Social Conditions. Rapid Reports, 1991/4

EUROSTAT (1990)
La pauvreté en chiffres. L'Europe au début des années '80. Bruxelles

FEANTSA (1993)
Basic Statistics on Homelessness in Europe. Internal Documentation, FEANTSA, Brussels

FERRERA, M. (1993)
EC Citizens and Social Protection: main results from a Eurobarometer survey. CCE DGV/E/2, Brussels

FIERENS, J. (1993)
Droit et exclusion en Belgique. Rapport présenté à la Commission des Communautés Européennes, DG V, Bruxelles

FIERENS, J. (1992)
Droit et pauvreté. Droits de l'homme, sécurité sociale, aide sociale. Bruylant, Bruxelles

FIERENS, J. (1995)
Communication for FEANTSA, Brussels

FILOSA, F. (1993)
Vite Perdute per Strada, Storie di barboni d'oggi. Franco Muzzio Editore, Padova

FNARS (1995)
Accueil, héberger, insérer, L'Echo de la FNARS, 26 Janvier 1995

FNARS (1994)
Face a l'urgence sociale, amplifier la mobilisation. l'Echo de la FNARS, Novembre 1994

FOURASTIE, J. (1959)
De la vie traditionelle à la vie tertiaire. Recherches sur le calendrier démographique de l'homme moyen, **Population**, 3

FONDATIONS (1995)
Les Sans-Abri. **Fondations** No. 1 January

FROMM, E. (1956)
To Have or to Be? Harper and Row, New York

HAMILTON, W.D. (1964)
The General Evolution of Social Behaviour, I & II. **Journal of Theoretical Biology**, 7, 1-52

HARDOY, J., D. SATERTHWAITE (1989)
Squatter Citizen. Life in the Urban Third World. Earthscan Publications Ltd. London

HARVEY, B. (1995)
The Use of Legislation to Address a Social Problem: The Example of the Housing Act, 1988. **Administration**, Vol. 43, No.1, 76-85

HARVEY, B. (1994A)
The Right to Housing and Housing Policy in Europe. Conference on Homeless in Germany - Civil and Human Rights are Invisible, Braunschweig, 16 October 1991

HARVEY, B. (1994B)
Europe's Homeless People and the Role of Housing. Workshop on Housing - Social Integration and Exclusion, Copenhagen, 16 May 1994

HENDESSI, M. (1992)
4 in 10. Report on Young Women Who Became Homeless as a Result of Sexual Abuse. CHAR, London

HEYDENDAEL, P.H.J.M., M.H.R. NUY, H.G. BROUWERS (1990)
Plott. Rapport eerste fase. Instituut voor Sociale Geneeskunde, Nijmegen

HOFFMANN-NOWOTNY, H.J. (1987)
The Future of the Family. Plenaries. European Population Conference, Central Statistical Office of Finland

HOUSING POLICY DEBATE (1991)
Fannie Mae Annual Housing Conference May 14, 1991, **Housing Policy Debate** Volume 2, Issue 3

INGLEHART, R. (1990)
Culture Shifts in Advance Industrial Society. Princeton University Press, Princeton

INGLEHART, R. (1977)
The Silent Revolution - Changing Values and Political Styles Among Western Publics. Princeton University Press, Princeton

INSEE (1988,1992)
Enquites logement. INSE, Paris

INTERNATIONAL LABOUR ORGANIZATION (1961)
Recommendation 115 on Worker's Housing. ILO Governing Body

IRIS (1993)
Huisvesting in Brussel. Een beschouwing over het geval van de tweede verblijven, Schaut C., N. van Droogenbroeck, BRES Nr. 14 **IRIS Uitgaven**, Brussel

IRIS (1993)
Impact van de huurprijzen op de koopkracht van de Brusselse bevolking. Degadt, J., M. Cottyn. BRES Nr. 16, **IRIS Uitgaven**, Brussel

ISTAT (1993)
Notizie sulle condizioni abitative delle famiglie desunte dall'indagine sui consumi delle famiglie 1992. Roma

JENCKS, C. (1993)
The Homeless. Harvard University Press, Cambridge

KLIMOP (1994)
Computerized Registration System Used by Service Providers from January 1, 1994

KNOWLES, E.S. (1979)
The Proximity of Others: A Critique of Crowding Research and Integration with Social Sciences. **Journal of Population**, 2

KOEGEL, P., M.A. BURNAM (1988)
Alcoholism among homeless adults in the inner city of Los Angeles. **Archives of General Psychiatry**, 45, 1011-1018

LAFORE, R. (1993)
Droit au logement et mutations sociales. A la recherche des concepts, **Vie Sociale**, CEDIAS 5-6/1993, 5-25

LAUSSINOTTE, S. (1994)
L'expulsion. De la reconnaissance du droit au logement à la réalité des sans-logis. ISA éditions, Paris

LESTHAEGHE, R., G. MOORS (1990)
Rationality, Cohort and Reproduction. Conference Paper, Fondazione Giovanni Agnelli, Firenze

LINKE, W. (1988)
Changes in Household Structures in Europe. European Population Committee, CDPO (88) 3, Council of Europe, Strasbourg

LOUVOT, C. (1992)
Projections of the Number of Households in France to the Year 2010 and the Medium-term Consequences for Housing Requirements. In: UNITED NATIONS, **Changing Population Age Structure, 1990-2015, Demographic and Economic Consequences and Implications**. United Nations, Geneva

MARQUES BALSA, C. J. BARRETO (1994)
Sans-Abri au Portugal. FEANTSA, Brussels

MASLOW, A. (1970)
Motivation and Personality. Harper and Row, New York

MATTHIESEN, P. (1988)
Family and Cohabitation. Paper presented at the Seminar Population Trends and Population Policy, Inter-University Centre, Dubrovnik

MCCARTHY, P. (1988)
A Study of the Work Skills, Experience and Preferences of Simon Community Residents. Simon Community, Dublin

MÉDICINS SANS FRONTIÉRES (1993)
Les sans-abri. Socialement maudits - Médicalement oubliés.
Forum de Lutte contre la Pauvreté, Bruxelles

MISSOC (1993)
Social Protection in the Member States of the Community, Situation on July 1st 1993 and Evolution. Commission of the European Communities, DG V, Brussels

MOORS, H., R. PALOMBA (EDS.) (1995)
Population, Family and Welfare, A Comparative Survey of European Attitudes, Volume 1. Clarendon Press, Oxford

NASCIMENTO, F. (1993)
Homelessness in Portugal. FEANTSA, Brussels

NUY, M., L. SMITS (1992)
Views of Homelessness. FEANTSA, Brussels

O'HIGGENS, M., S. JENKINS
Poverty in the EC 1975, 1980, 1985. In: Teekens, R., B.M.S. Van Praag (Eds.), **Analysing Poverty in the European Community, Policy issues, research options and data sources**. Eurostat News Special Edition 1

O'SULLIVAN, E. (1994)
Homelessness, Housing Policy and Exclusion in the Republic of Ireland. FEANTSA, Brussels

OLIVER, Q. (1992)
Housing: Discussion Paper. Colloquy Proceedings, Towards Greater Social Justice in Europe, The Challenge of Marginalization and Poverty, Council of Europe, Strasbourg, 3-5 December 1991

PARKE, R.D., D.B. SAWIN (1979)
Children's Privacy in the Home. **Environment and Behaviour**, 11

PELTS, M., A. WAGNER (1994)
Rapport 1994 pour l'Observatoire de la FEANTSA:. Grand-Duché de Luxembourg. FEANTSA, Bruxelles

PRÉEL, B. (1992)
Les sans abri: état des lieux. Rapport pour le groupe SCIC à partir du cecenssement de 1990-1992, BIPE

PRIEMUS, H. (1992)
Housing Indicators. In: Executive Survey of the Housing Indicators Program

RANDALL, G. (1992)
Counted out: an investigation into the extent of single homelessness outside London. CHAR, London

RENARD, R., G. VAN MENXEL (1992)
Les sans-abri en Europe. FEANTSA, Bruxelles

RENARD, R. (1994)
Sans-abri en Belgique. FEANTSA, Brussels

ROSTGAARD, T., I. KOCH-NIELSEN (1994)
Homelessness and Social Exclusion in Denmark. FEANTSA, Brussels

ROWNTREE, B.S. (1901)
Poverty: A Study of Town Life. MacMillan

RUHSTRAT, E., V. BUSCH-GEERTSEMA (1994)
Armut und Wohnungslosigkeit. Entstehung und Verlauf von Wohnungslosigkeit. In: KOCH, F., C. REIS (Hrsg.), **Wohnungspolitik in sozialpolitischer Perspektive**, Frankfurt a. Main

RUHSTRAT, E., V. BUSCH-GEERTSEMA (1994)
Wohnungsnotfalle sicherung der wohnungsversorgung fur wirtschaftlich oder social benachteiligte haushalte. Im aufrag der bundesministerien fur raumordnung, bauwesen und stadtebau und fur familie und senioren. Vorgelegt vor der Gesellscaft fur Innovative Socialforschung und Sozialplanung e.V., Bremen

RUSHTON, P.J. (1980)
Altruism, Socialization and Society. Printice-Hall, Inc. Englewood Cliffs, New Jersey

SACHAR, R. (1992)

The Realisation of Economic, Social and Cultural Rights: The Right to Adequate Housing. Working Paper, United Nations Economic and Social Council, E/CN.4/Sub.2/1992/15

SAKAIYA, T. (1991)

The Knowledge-Value Revolution, or a History of the Future. Bellew Publishing, London

SALICATH, N., H. THOMSEN (1992)

Homelessness in Denmark., FEANTSA, Brussels

SALINAS RAMOS, F. (1994)

Sans-abri en Espagne, Observatoire National des Sans-Abri en Espagne. FEANTSA, Brussels

SALINAS RAMOS, F. (1993)

Homelessness in Spain. FEANTSA, Brussels

SAPOUNAKIS, A. (1994)

Annual Report on Homelessness and Substandard Housing Conditions in Greece. FEANTSA, Brussels

SAPOUNAKIS, A. (1993)

Homelessness in Greece, FEANTSA, Brussels

SATTERTHWAITE, D. (1995)

Rapid Urbanization and the Urban Environment. **Proceeding of the Seminar on Demography and Poverty**. IUSSP, March 2-4 1995, Florence

SEN A. (1995)

Mortality as an Indicator of Economic Success and Failure. Innocenti Lecture given at the UNICEF-IUSSP conference Demography and Poverty, March 3, Florence

SHELTER (1989)

Housing Britain: Let's Get to Work. London

SHiL - Single Homeless in London (1992)
Silt-up or move on? Housing London's Single Homeless. Spaull
S. SHiL/Association of London Authorities, London

SPECHT-KITTLER, T. (1994)
**Housing Poverty in a Rich Society: Houselessness and Unaccept-
able Housing Conditions in Germany.** FEANTSA, Brussels

SPECHT-KITTLER, T. (1993)
National Report on Homelessness in Germany. FEANTSA, Brussels

THUISLOZENZORG VLAANDEREN (1993)
Klientgegevens. Antwerpen

TOSI, A., C. RANCI (1994)
Homelessness in Italy, 1994 Report. FEANTSA, Brussels

TOSI, A., C. RANCI (1993)
Homeless People in Italy. FEANTSA, Brussels

TRIVERS, R.L. (1971)
The Evolution of Reciprocal Altruism. **Quart. Rev. Biol.** 46, 1,
35-57

TURNER, J.F.C. (1976)
Housing by People: Towards Autonomy in Building Environment.
Marion Boyards Publishers Ltd., London

UNITED NATIONS (1993)
Draft Declaration on the Rights of Indigenous Peoples as
referred to in : The Human Right to Adequate Housing Fact Sheet
No. 21

UNITED NATIONS (1992)
The right to adequate housing. Working paper submitted by Rajin-
dar Sachar to the Commission on Human Rights,
E/CN.4/Sub.2/1992/15

UNITED NATIONS (1991)
Promoting the realization of the right to adequate housing.
Sub-Commission of Prevention of Discrimination and Protection
of Minorities, resolution 1991/26

UNITED NATIONS (1990)
**International Convention of the Protection of the Rights of All
Migrant Workers and Members of their Families.** General Assembly resolution 45/158

UNITED NATIONS (1989)
Convention on the Rights of the Child. General Assembly resolution 44/25

UNITED NATIONS (1986)
Declaration on the Right to Development (1986) General Assembly resolution 41/128

UNITED NATIONS (1979)
**Convention on the Elimination of All Forms of Discrimination
Against Women.** General Assembly resolution 34/180

UNITED NATIONS (1976)
Vancouver Declaration on Human Settlement. United Nations
Conference on Human Settlement

UNITED NATIONS (1969)
Declaration on Social Progress and Development. General Assembly resolution 2542 (XXIV)

UNITED NATIONS (1966)
International Covenant on Economic, Social and Cultural Rights.
General Assembly resolution 2200 A (XXI)

UNITED NATIONS (1965)
**International Convention on the Elimination of All Forms of
Racial Discrimination**. General Assembly resolution 2106 A (XX)

UNITED NATIONS (1959)
Declaration of the Rights of the Child. General Assembly resolution 1386 (XIV)

UNITED NATIONS (1951)
Convention Relating to the Status of Refugees. United Nations Conference of Plenipotentiaries of the Status of Refugees and Stateless Persons

UNITED NATIONS (1948)
Universal Declaration of Human Rights. United Nations General Assembly

VOGEL-POLSKY, E. (1992)
Rapport sul l'intégration des droits sociaux fondamentaux dans l'ordre juridique communautaire: Une stratégie de renforcement de la garantie des droits des personnes les plus démunies. Rapport préliminaire présenté à la Commission des Communautés Européennes, DGV, Bruxelles

VRANKEN, J., G. VAN MENXEL (1994)
Social Exclusion in Belgium, Consolidated Report 1991-1994 for the European Observatory on Policies to Combat Social Exclusion. University of Antwerp

VRANKEN, J. (1972)
Armoede in België. De Nederlandse Boekhandel, Antwerpen

WALKER, A. (1994)
Observatories and the Social Debate at European Level. Paper presented at the Symposium European Community and the Social Sphere, 2-4 June, Paris

WRIGHT, R. (1994)
Household structure and poverty. **Genus**, Volume L, Luglio-Dicembre 1994, N. 3-4

APPENDIX 1

OBSERVATORY CONTRIBUTORS

NETWORK OF
NATIONAL CORRESPONDENTS IN 1994

BELGIUM

Roland RENARD   Rue des Savoyards 29
                                  B-1495 Villers-la-Ville

DENMARK

Inger KOCH-NIELSEN   Danish National Institute of
                                  Social Research
                                  Borgergade 28
                                  DK-1300 Copenhagen K

GERMANY

Thomas SPECHT-KITTLER   BAG für Wohnungslosenhilfe
                                  Postfach 13 01 48
                                  D-33544 Bielefeld

FRANCE

Anne DE GOUY

F.N.A.R.S.
C/o Habitat Educatif
101 rue Talma
F-94400 Vitry-sur-Seine

SPAIN

Francisco SALINAS RAMOS

CARITAS ESPAÑOLA
San Bernardo 99bis 7
E-28015 Madrid

GREECE

Aristidis SAPOUNAKIS

9 Angelou Pyrri Street
GR-115 27 Athens

IRELAND

Eoin O'SULLIVAN

Streetwise National Coalition
Upper Sherrard Street 26
IRL-Dublin 1

ITALY

Antonio TOSI

Politecnico di Milano
Facolta di Architectura
Via Bonardi 3
I- 20133 MILANO

LUXEMBOURG

Alain WAGNER

CNDS
B.P. 65
L-7201 Walferdange

NETHERLANDS

Hendrik Jan DE FEIJTER   University of Amsterdam
Dept of Physical Planning and
Demography
Nieuwe Prinsengracht 130
NL-1018 VZ Amsterdam

PORTUGAL

Casimiro MARQUES BALSA   University of Lisbon
Dept of Sociology
26-C Av de Berna
P-1000 Lisboa

UNITED KINGDOM

Barbra CARLISLE   Shelter
88 Old Street
UK-London EC1V 9HU

Robert ALDRIDGE   Scottish Council for Single
Homeless
Forrest Road 9
UK-Edinburgh EH1 2QH

SCIENTIFIC COMMITTEE

Mary DALY   Georg-August-Universität Göttingen
                         ZENS
                         Center for European and North American Studies
                         Humbotallee 3
                         D- 37073 GÖTTINGEN
                         Germany

Jan VRANKEN   Universiteit Antwerpen
                         Prinsestraat 13
                         B-2000 ANTWERPEN
                         Belgium

Antonio TOSI   Politecnico di Milano
                         Facolta di Architectura
                         Via Bonardi 3
                         I- 20133 MILAN
                         Italy

Jacques FIERENS   Faculté des sciences économiques et sociales
                         Rempart de la Vierge, 8
                         B-5000 NAMUR
                         Belgium

APPENDIX 2

PUBLICATIONS OF FEANTSA

BOUDRU, F. (1992)
Une première approche européenne des politiques spécifiques et des actions en faveur des sans-abri. First report of the European Observatory on Homelessness. FEANTSA, Bruxelles, 78 pages.

DALY, M. (1992)
Homeless People in Europe - The Rising Tide. Summary report of the European Observatory on Homelessness. FEANTSA, Brussels, 27 pages.

RENARD, R., G. VAN MENXEL (1993)
Les Sans-Abri en Europe - Analyse comparative de la situation des sans-abri dans les Etats membres de la Communauté Européenne : définitions et actions, ampleur, caractéristiques et causes. Second report of the European Observatory on Homelessness. FEANTSA, Bruxelles, 80 pages.

DALY, M. (1993)
Abandoned : Profile of Europe's Homeless People. Summary report of the European Observatory on Homelessness. FEANTSA, Brussels, 23 pages.

DRAKE, M. (1994)
Homeless people in Europe and their rights". Third report of the European Observatory on Homelessness. FEANTSA, Brussels, 53 pages.

DALY, M. (1994)
The Right to a Home, the Right to a Future. Summary report of the European Observatory on Homelessness. FEANTSA, Brussels, 25 pages.

AVRAMOV, D. (1994)
Homelessness : a Condition or a Social Process? An overview for the 12 Member States of the European Union. Working Document, FEANTSA, Brussels, 29 pages.

National reports for 1993 [1]

RENARD, R. (1993)
Sans-abri en Belgique. FEANTSA, Bruxelles.

KOCH-NIELSEN, I. (1993)
Homelessness in Denmark. FEANTSA, Brussels.

SPECHT-KITTLER, T. (1993)
Homelessness in Germany. FEANTSA, Brussels.

SALINAS RAMOS, F. (1993)
Homeless in Spain. FEANTSA, Brussels.

DE GOUY, A. (1993)
Observatoire des sans-abri: France. FEANTSA, Bruxelles.

SAPOUNAKIS, A. (1993)
National report on homelessness in Greece. FEANTSA, Brussels.

O'SULLIVAN, E. (1993)
The nature of homelessness in the Republic of Ireland. FEANTSA, Brussels.

TOSI, A., C. RANCI (1993)
Homeless in Italy. FEANTSA, Brussels.

---

[1]   Available for consultation at FEANTSA's secretariat.

WAGNER, A., M. PELS (1993)
Sans-abri au Luxembourg. FEANTSA, Bruxelles.

NUY, M. (1993)
The legal and social reality of homeless in The Netherlands.
FEANTSA, Brussels.

NASCIMENTO, F. (1993)
Sans-abri au Portugal. FEANTSA, Bruxelles.

ASHCROFT, S. (1993)
Homelessness in England and Wales. FEANTSA, Brussels.

HAMILTON, S. (1993)
Homeless in Northern Ireland. FEANTSA, Brussels.

ALDRIDGE, R. (1993)
Homelessness in Scotland. FEANTSA, Brussels.

National reports for 1994

RENARD, R. (1994)
Sans-abri en Belgique. FEANTSA, Bruxelles.

ROSTGAARD, T., I. KOCH-NIELSEN (1994)
Homelessness and Social Exclusion in Denmark. FEANTSA,
Brussels.

SPECHT-KITTLER, T. (1994)
**Housing Poverty in a rich Society : Houselessness and
unnacceptable housing condition in Germany. A new perspective
on homelessness**. FEANTSA, Brussels.

DE GOUY, A. (1994)
Sans-abri en France. FEANTSA, Bruxelles.

SALINAS RAMOS, F. (1994)
Sans-abri en Espagne. FEANTSA, Bruxelles.

SAPOUNAKIS, A. (1994)
Homelessness in Greece. FEANTSA, Brussels.

O'SULLIVAN, E. (1994)
Homelesness, housing policy and exclusion in the Republic of Ireland. FEANTSA, Brussels.

TOSI, A., C. RANCI (1994)
Homelessness in Italy. FEANTSA, Brussels.

PELS,M., A. WAGNER (1994)
Sans-abri au Luxembourg. FEANTSA, Bruxelles.

DE FEIJTER, H., H. RADSTAAK (1994)
Homelessness in the Netherlands. FEANTSA, Brussels.

MARQUES BALSA, C., J. BARRETO (1994)
Sans-abri au Portugal. FEANTSA, Bruxelles.

CARLISLE, B. (1994)
Homelessness in the United Kingdom. FEANTSA, Brussels.